VEGAN RAMEN

# VEGAN RAMEN

## 50 PLANT-BASED RECIPES FOR RAMEN AT HOME

Armon Pakdel and Zoe Lichlyter

Photography by Elysa Weitala

ROCKRIDGE PRESS

For general information on our other products and services or to obtain technical support, please contact our Customer Care Department within the United States at (866) 744-2665, or outside the United States at (510) 253-0500.

Rockridge Press publishes its books in a variety of electronic and print formats. Some content that appears in print may not be available in electronic books, and vice versa.

TRADEMARKS: Rockridge Press and the Rockridge Press logo are trademarks or registered trademarks of Callisto Media Inc. and/or its affiliates, in the United States and other countries, and may not be used without written permission. All other trademarks are the property of their respective owners. Rockridge Press is not associated with any product or vendor mentioned in this book.

Interior and Cover Designer: Jennifer Hsu
Art Producer: Sara Feinstein
Editor: Georgia Freedman
Production Editor: Jenna Dutton
Production Manager: Holly Haydash

Photography © 2021 Elysa Weitala. Food styling by Victoria Woollard. Illustration used under license from Shutterstock.com. Author photo courtesy of Tom Healy.

Paperback ISBN: 978-1-63807-121-1
eBook ISBN: 978-1-63807-171-6
R0

DEDICATED TO OUR
RESPECTIVE GRANDMOTHERS,
MOKARAM AND NARUMI.

# CONTENTS

———

# INTRODUCTION

We are Zoe and Armon, the owners of Safframen, a food cart in Portland, Oregon, serving exclusively plant-based ramen. It is one of only a handful of fully plant-based ramen restaurants in the world.

Zoe (pronounced Zō) is part Japanese, and Armon is part Persian, and the menu at Safframen incorporates aspects of both of our cultural heritages (skewing heavily toward the Japanese side). Like most cuisines, Japanese and Iranian foods both have histories that are inextricably linked to the use of animal products. Beef and lamb are staples of Iranian cuisine, and seafood is ubiquitous in Japan.

When we made the decision to open Safframen in 2019, we were faced with a daunting task: to serve high-quality ramen without using animal proteins. In spite of the rising popularity of high-quality meat alternatives, the negative stigma surrounding vegan food still lingers. We felt an obligation to create recipes that avoided animal products but could still impress our immigrant grandparents. We were not going to compromise. We dove deep, honed our skills, tweaked our recipes, and strived to live up to our own standards.

Our food cart became a modest success, thanks in no small part to the fact that Portland, where we live, has a large vegan population, and these adventurous eaters tend to go out on a limb for a new plant-based business. During this time, we also began to notice an overwhelming interest in vegan ramen—and a serious lack of available resources for cooks to prepare it. Popular recipes for plant-based ramens tended to feel compromised and didn't fully live up to their conventional counterparts. As we developed our own recipes, we realized that this problem was actually a blessing in disguise, as it forced us to invent our own solutions to the problems we encountered.

This book is a direct expansion of the ideas we developed for our food cart. As we've grown and evolved, we have been able to tackle many of the questions that have challenged us from the beginning: How do you make tonkotsu ramen that is as rich and delicious as the version with pork in it? How do you achieve the sublime simplicity of a bowl of shio ramen without bonito flakes? With much time and work, we developed recipes that answer these questions.

We have no qualms about sharing the knowledge we've accumulated. No clinging to closely guarded secrets for us—we prefer a world abundant with great vegan ramen! In this book, we'll share what we've learned over years of study and experimentation: First, we'll take a brief look at the history of ramen culture. Once we are steeped in context, we examine what it means to make ramen *plant-based*.

The recipes start with the components that comprise ramen as a dish: oil, tare, broth, noodles, and toppings. Master these building blocks, and making a bowl of ramen becomes a far more approachable task.

Then we have our ramen recipes: 24 dishes, each of which usually utilizes one of each of the five previously outlined components. (Once you've prepped the components in advance, cooking ramen is mostly a matter of assembly.) Some of the dishes in this book are vegan versions of Japanese classics, while others are more inventive and draw on our own personal histories and cultural touchstones as well as the wisdom we've gained from the day-to-day work of running a ramen food cart.

Lastly, we'll round out our recipes with some delicious sides to serve alongside your bowls.

When we began our own vegan ramen journey, we often wished we had a guide like this one. We want vegan ramen to be a dish that stands on its own merits—not a subpar duplication but a unique category on par with any other style of ramen. With this book as your guide, we hope to bring you into our world and give you the tools to flourish into a great vegan ramen chef.

# PART ONE

# STEP-BY-STEP VEGAN RAMEN

The first step to understanding how to make vegan ramen is to look at ramen's history, its cultural importance, and its evolution. After that, we'll dissect the elements of ramen, assessing each component, identifying its purpose, and working through how to build up to a full bowl.

Once we understand the elements of ramen (and start to think about how to use these elements in a vegan context), we'll develop our base recipes—the broths, flavorings, toppings, and handmade noodles that we'll use as the building blocks of the recipes in the latter part of the book.

# CHAPTER 1
# GETTING TO KNOW VEGAN RAMEN

Consider the first chapter of this book an orientation—Ramen 101. We cover many basic questions: What is ramen? What is it made of? Where did it come from? What is its history, and why does it matter? The answers pave the way toward tackling the challenge tied to this book's premise: how to create delicious vegan ramen.

As the adage goes, to break the rules, you must first know the rules. Breaking free of the conventions of traditional ramen, which are deeply tied to both animal products and Japanese tradition, while simultaneously honoring the principles that make ramen great, will be a challenge. To pull this off, a deeper understanding of ramen's past is the key we need to unlock its plant-based future.

# ALL ABOUT RAMEN

At its most basic level, ramen is noodle soup.

Of course, it is much more than *just* noodle soup. Delightfully savory and filling, ramen has an international reputation. It has soared in popularity over the last several decades, and it now rivals sushi as Japan's top culinary export. For anyone who has had ramen before, it's not difficult to see why; from the moment you sit down with your bowl to the very last slurp, the act of eating ramen is a uniquely intense, and even hypnotic, experience.

At the sight of glistening oil and bright yellow noodles bobbing in steaming broth, you accept that such beauty is ephemeral. As you slurp your way through the bowl, temperatures cool, flavors intermingle, and, by the final bite, your meal has evolved into something entirely different from what it was when you began. Such is the sophistication of ramen, the primary trick by which it works its magic. This transformative quality is a definitive part of the experience.

## RAMEN CULTURE

Ramen's reputation is well earned, both inside and outside of Japan, where the dish was originally developed. In Japan, ramen is served and eaten with haste. In spite of its notoriously long preparation time, ramen is considered a "fast food." Japanese workers often stop for ramen in subway stations during work commutes and consume their bowls with great speed, not only to prevent the noodles from getting soggy but also to make sure they don't miss their trains.

But ramen isn't just for commuters. After a long day of work, what could be better than a piping-hot bowl of tonkotsu at the local *ramen-ya*? In Tokyo, late-night dining is synonymous with ramen, as there are a plethora of 24-hour ramen shops all over the city. There are options for everybody—from chain restaurants and local dives for a comfortable fix to upscale establishments pushing creative limits. And even with all the dine-out options, ramen is still a popular homemade family dinner.

Many people in Japan also enjoy eating their ramen inside a "focus booth," a narrow, isolated stall where you're shielded on either side from other diners by opaque shutters, often alienated even from your server by an automated menu system. The purpose of a focus booth is to block out distractions, allowing you to give your (literal) complete focus to the bowl of ramen before you.

# RAMEN HISTORY

For most of the 17th, 18th, and 19th centuries, Japan was a self-isolated island nation, trading sparsely with the rest of the world. However, in the 1850s (after a US commander sailed into Tokyo Harbor with a fleet of warships), the country opened up to trade, resulting in a rapid transition from feudalism to industrialization. When this happened, new ideas, products, and foods flooded into the islands.

A few decades earlier, in China, a style of hand-pulled noodles was invented in the Hui Muslim community. It was called *lamian* ("la" = "pulled," "mian" = "noodles"). After Japan opened up, these lamian noodles made their way to its shores. Their name was localized to "ramen."

By the early 20th century, ramen had become popular in Japanese port towns. Noodle men pulled portable carts, blowing horns to announce their presence and stopping to cook up a cheap and filling meal for workers. Japanese cooks were already used to enjoying bowls of buckwheat soba noodles, which were sometimes served with a light broth. The texture of the new ramen noodles—heavier, chewier, and made of wheat flour—worked well with these same, familiar flavors.

During World War II, eating ramen was discouraged. Nationalist messages urged Japanese citizens to consume rice, the traditional staple grain, and not foreign wheat. As the war intensified, imperial control tightened, and ramen was essentially outlawed, available only through Yakuza black markets.

After the war, however, the United States brought imported foods, like wheat, to the islands as part of the Government Aid and Relief in Occupied Areas program. The infusion of affordable American wheat made ramen (and other wheat-based foods) even more popular than they were before the war.

In 1958, a Taiwanese businessman living in Japan named Momofuku Ando introduced instant ramen to the Japanese market. Though technically not the first food of its kind (Matsuda Sangyo made a version several years earlier that failed to sell), and not nearly as dirt cheap as it would eventually become, these flash-fried noodle bricks and seasoning packets were a massive success and quickly became a Japanese pantry staple. The incredible popularity of instant ramen represented a new benchmark for ramen. Outside of Japan, it would become many eaters' introduction to the dish.

In the mid-1980s, a culinary renaissance began, as chefs invented and popularized new forms of ramen. This was the start of ramen's elevation from street food to serious culinary heavyweight. In 2004, Korean American chef David Chang opened Momofuku ramen bar in New York City. Until that point, for most Americans, the word "ramen" had been interchangeable with instant ramen. Momofuku (named after the pioneering ramen food scientist) was the beginning of the legitimization of ramen in America.

Since then, ramen's popularity as a culinary phenomenon has grown exponentially. Today, great ramen restaurants can be found not just in Japan and the United States but all over the world, as chefs from a variety of backgrounds play with the classics, bringing them into inventive new territories. Thanks to these developments, there has never been a better time to be a ramen lover.

# Anatomy of a Bowl

Ramen is composed of five core components: broth, tare, oil, noodles, and toppings:

**Broth:** The liquid part of the soup is where a myriad of savory components are concentrated.

**Tare:** This concentrated flavor base (the name translates to "sauce" in Japanese) contains much of a bowl's saltiness and complexity. On its own, it can be used as a dipping sauce or a glaze (think teriyaki). In ramen, it combines with the broth.

**Oil:** Flavored oils provide a strong aroma and allow the broth's flavor to cling to the noodles.

**Ramen Noodles:** The soup's primary carbohydrate (and the ingredient it is named for) provides a chewy texture and a vehicle to carry all other flavors.

**Toppings:** Cooked foods and garnishes add a variety of flavors and textures to finished bowls of ramen.

Each of the components listed above is made in a separate process, and they are added together in quick succession when a bowl is ready to be assembled. Here is a simplified guide to making your first bowl of ramen:

First, find a deep bowl. Add a small amount of aromatic oil to the bowl. Then mix in the tare, incorporating it with the oil. Add in boiling broth, whisking gently so the oil and tare continue to integrate. Have your noodles cooked and ready when the broth is poured into the bowl. Carefully add the noodles to the bowl. Garnish with toppings, serve, and enjoy!

## TYPES OF RAMEN

Ramen is a food defined by its evolution, dancing through various cultures and subcultures, adapting to whatever conditions demanded of it. This food, which began as a Japanese riff on a Chinese noodle soup, was entirely absorbed into Japanese culture and then continued to change with the times. Over the decades, a variety of popular ramen types have emerged. Armed with a basic understanding of ramen's five core components (see Anatomy of a Bowl, page 6), we can begin to understand what differentiates each type. Let's begin with the four most popular types (or "supertypes," as we like to call them): shio, shoyu, miso, and tonkotsu.

Shio, shoyu, and miso are defined by their tare component. Tonkotsu, on the other hand, is defined by its rich broth. The distinctions between the different types of ramen can be muddled, as there is much overlap between their ingredients and preparation. However, for our purposes, they can more or less be categorized this way:

**Shio:** Ramen with salt tare. It often contains a lighter broth with acidic notes. Due to the neutral taste of salt, shio is one of the most flexible and adaptable styles.

**Shoyu:** Ramen with soy sauce tare. This is the original type of ramen and often is built to evoke more classic Japanese flavor profiles.

**Miso:** Ramen with miso tare, i.e., one made with fermented soybean paste. This is a popular base for heavier bowls with richer and more intense flavors.

**Tonkotsu:** A thick, creamy type of ramen that uses a stock made from pork bones.

## REGIONAL RAMEN

Aside from these four ramen supertypes, there are a plethora of regional variations. Here are some of the most popular:

**Mazemen:** A Taiwanese-inspired brothless ramen invented by Menya Hanabi in Nagoya. The name means "mixed noodle." Instead of broth, the ingredients are mixed thoroughly with the tare and served cold.

**Tsukemen:** Ramen with the broth and noodles served separately. The noodles are thicker than average and designed to be dipped in the broth. This version was pioneered by Kazuo Yamagishi in Tokyo.

**Tantanmen:** This is a Japanese adaptation of dan dan noodles—a dish that originated in China's Sichuan province. The most familiar tantanmen recipes are based on the Hong Kong version of dan dan, which includes soup, rather than the brothless version from Sichuan.

**Hiyashi Chuka:** Translating to "chilled Chinese," this is another brothless ramen, and a summer favorite. It is dressed in sesame oil and soy sauce and served chilled. It is not unlike a noodle salad. This variety originated in Sendai, a city just north of Tokyo.

**Kimchi Ramen:** This ramen embraces the flavors of Korean kimchi—spicy fermented peppers, napa cabbage, carrots, and daikon radish. This is a newer style of ramen, and no one is quite sure if it originated among Korean immigrants living in Japan or in South Korea, where ramen is also popular.

**Tonyu:** Ramen using soy milk in its savory soup base. Tonyu ramen shows the endless versatility of soy. It is difficult to find information on the origins of this style, but it can sometimes be found on menus as a vegetarian or vegan option.

## MAKING RAMEN VEGAN

Now we arrive at our first challenge in making plant-based ramen: Ramen, throughout its history, has been made from ingredients derived from animals, including pork bones, chicken stock, gelatin, fish flakes, fish *cakes*, and so on. For anyone approaching the challenge of creating plant-based ramen, it is clearly a far more complicated task than swapping a topping or two. Ramen does not simply utilize meat as a garnish. In fact, ramen is often *constructed at its foundation* to maximize the potential of such products.

Many vegans understand that, when adapting meat-based cuisines, one-for-one substitutes won't always cut it. To compromise in this fashion is to accept inferiority. For those who seek to treat vegan cuisine seriously, there is something to prove in the creation of a bowl of plant-based ramen. It is complicated, requiring a demanding attention to detail. Much like the pioneering ramen chefs who transformed this savory noodle soup from college-dorm staple to fine dining all-star, we vegan chefs feel obligated to *elevate* plant-based ramen into its own unique and legitimate category. Just as cart-hauling cooks adapted "lamian" into "ramen," as Momofuku Ando turned ramen into instant ramen, and as David Chang elevated the noodles for New York diners, we, too, are paving our own way.

If we cannot just substitute ingredients, where do we begin? The goal of this book is to answer that question.

# YOUR VEGAN RAMEN PANTRY

There are some key tools and ingredients you'll need to make vegan ramen. We've done our best to include ingredients that can usually be found at either conventional grocery stores or large Asian grocery stores. Many markets in the United States have Asian ingredients sections that can also be useful.

## DRY AND SHELF-STABLE GOODS

Many of the specialty ingredients you'll need to make vegan ramen are shelf-stable. You can stock up on them (either at an Asian market or from an online retailer) and then have them on hand whenever you need them.

**Bread Flour:** If you're making your own ramen noodles, you'll need a flour with a high gluten content, which gives the noodles their signature bouncy, chewy quality. We recommend King Arthur brand bread flour with 12.7 percent gluten.

**Canola Oil:** You'll need a plain, unflavored oil to use as a base for oil infusions. Canola oil is our preferred choice, but vegetable oil (aka soybean oil), avocado oil, grapeseed oil, and rice bran oil will work just fine. (Avoid extra-virgin olive oil or unrefined coconut oil, which have their own strong flavors.)

**Cornstarch:** Starch is necessary during noodle making, as it prevents the noodles from sticking. A light dusting of starch goes a long way. Potato starch, tapioca starch, arrowroot powder, and rice flour all work as well.

**Dried Shiitake Mushrooms:** Shiitake mushrooms are loaded with umami flavor and make an excellent stock base. Any kind of dried mushrooms will work—porcini, portobello, maitake, and so on. We tend to stick with shiitake due to their widespread use within Japanese cuisine.

**Dry Noodles:** While fresh ramen noodles will always have the best texture (see page 47), dried noodles can function as a good stand-in. Fortunately, almost all dry noodles are vegan; manufacturers typically reserve eggs for fresh noodle products.

You can use a variety of different types of dried noodles for ramen, depending on how committed you are to re-creating restaurant-quality ramen. In a pinch, you can use flash-fried bricks of instant ramen. Any brand will do, although "cup" noodles will be trickier to separate from their containers. You can even use ordinary spaghetti noodles, though we recommend a slightly thicker variety (often labeled "thick spaghetti").

**Gochujang:** Korean fermented chili paste can be used in many of the same ways miso can in a bowl of ramen—but it offers an additional kick from the chilis it's made from. Brands like O'Food can often be found at supermarkets, but Korean grocery stores such as H Mart offer a wider variety to choose from.

**Kombu:** This dried seaweed is packed with glutamates. It is often sold as "dashi kombu." Don't confuse this product with the seaweed or nori used in sushi and other preparations—kombu comes in long, dried strips that are inedible until cooked. Our preferred brand for commercially available kombu is Wel-Pac.

**Mirin and Rice Vinegar:** Mirin and rice vinegar add important acidic notes to ramen tares. Any Asian-style rice vinegar will work here; just look for the unseasoned variety. Mirin, or rice cooking wine, is usually sweetened and has a syrup-like consistency. This sweetness gives it a gentler flavor than rice vinegar. (Kikkoman makes good staple versions of both ingredients.)

**Miso Paste:** Miso paste (made from fermented soybeans) is becoming increasingly available in regular supermarkets. It generally comes in three varieties—white, yellow, and red—and each has a different flavor. We recommend picking up a container of each to mix and match in your ramen.

**Mushroom Powder:** This is a potent glutamate hack and MSG substitute. (Glutamates are the amino acids that make food taste savory and rich.) Most mushroom powders are processed to remove the strong mushroom flavor, leaving only pure powdered savoriness. There are many varieties available, but the best only have a single ingredient on the label—mushrooms.

**Preserved Bamboo Shoots:** Bamboo shoots have a unique flavor and crunchy texture perfect for garnishing a bowl of ramen. They are usually canned. To use them, simply drain the brining liquid and add the shoots directly into your bowl, as a topping.

**Salt:** While salt is one of the most common cooking ingredients there is, it's important to be thoughtful about the type of salt you choose. Different varieties of salt contain very different levels of salinity and different textures. With ramen, we usually use flaky sea salt. Diamond Crystal kosher salt is also a go-to staple.

**Soy Curls:** These are a dried meat alternative product made from soy protein. We've found them significantly easier to cook with than TVP, another meat alternative made from the same stuff. A company called Butler produces a widely available brand of soy curls that, when marinated and cooked properly, can do a great job imitating the taste and texture of chicken. They are often sold in health-food stores and organic grocery stores such as Whole Foods.

**Soy Sauce:** While soy sauce is ubiquitous, most people buy only one kind, light soy sauce, which is thin and salty. We also use dark soy sauce, which is thicker and has a more complex taste. We even blend multiple soy sauces to balance our Shio Citrus Tare (page 33). (Tamari, which is similar to light soy sauce but is gluten-free, can also be used in many of our recipes.)

**Toasted Sesame Oil:** This aromatic oil is widely available. Most of the sesame oil sold in any market is the toasted type, even if it's not labeled as such. You'll recognize it by its darker brown color.

**Togarashi:** This Japanese dried chili seasoning is a great way to spice up your ramen bowl. This spice mix comes in two widely available varieties: ichimi togarashi, which is just pepper flakes, and shichimi togarashi, which also contains orange peel, sesame, and seaweed.

**White Pepper:** This is a staple Japanese spice that is similar to black pepper but significantly more pungent. Use it in small quantities to maximize the complexity of your tare. Pre-ground white pepper is commonly available, but if you can find whole white peppercorns and grind them yourself, the flavor will be even better.

## FRESH INGREDIENTS AND PRODUCE

Many of the vegetables we use to make our vegan ramen broths (and garnish our bowls) are common ingredients that can be found in any market. The soy products we use in place of meat toppings are also widely available.

**Bean Sprouts:** Soybean sprouts and mung bean sprouts both add a lovely, crunchy texture to your bowl. Soybean sprouts are distinguished by thick stems with golden beans on top, while mung bean sprouts are thinner, with green beans on their ends.

**Cabbage:** The humble cabbage is a kind of secret ingredient when it comes to adding umami to plant-based foods. We use standard green cabbage in broths, but for toppings, we like finely sliced savoy or Taiwanese cabbage.

**Fresh Shiitake Mushrooms:** Fresh shiitakes serve a purpose that's very different from their dried counterpart: simmered, seared, and seasoned, they have a meaty texture and a rich flavor that makes them a delicious ramen topping.

**Garlic:** Rich, pungent garlic creates wonderful infused oils. The flavor also helps replace some of the complex notes you would get from meat in traditional, non-vegan ramen.

**Ginger:** Fresh ginger, with its bitter and sweet notes, is a staple in Japanese cooking and an important ingredient for making several varieties of tare.

**Kabocha Squash:** When in season, this iconic Japanese winter squash is a perfect ramen topping. Bake it, fry it, sear it—there's no wrong way to go here. In the absence of fresh kabocha, other squash such as butternut makes a fine substitute.

**Scallions:** Also known as green onions, these are the sprouting shoots of onion bulbs. They're easier on the palate than the onions that grow under the ground. We usually slice them thin and use them as a garnish.

**Tofu:** Tofu is a protein made from coagulated soybean curds. It is infamously maligned as "bland"—any vegan or vegetarian is sure to have encountered this criticism. However, with 2,000 years of history and endless culinary applications, tofu can be absolutely delicious when used properly. Many kinds of tofu can be found in the refrigerated section of nearly every grocery store in America, but for the really good stuff, we recommend you visit a dedicated tofu shop, if you're lucky enough to live near one.

**Yellow Onions:** The standard onion is one of the best sources of plant glutamates. When we build our broths, we often use onions as a powerful base for our central flavor profiles.

# Don't Wait!

Preparing and eating ramen is a time-sensitive endeavor. With all the effort put into each component, the last thing you want is to drop cooked noodles into that hot broth, then realize you forgot to finish searing the mushrooms. By the time you do that, your noodles will be soggy. Making each element of your bowl at the right time, then assembling them properly, is the key to great ramen. Once your base ingredients and toppings are ready, you want to assemble your bowls quickly (and eat the finished ramen quickly, too). Here are a few tips to help you succeed:

1. As you're waiting for your broth and/or water to boil, preload your bowl with the oil and tare.

2. Boiling fresh ramen noodles should take a few minutes at most. If your noodles are done cooking sooner than you'd anticipated, halt the cooking process with a rinse of cold water in the sink *or* dunk them in a prepared bath of ice water. When you're ready to add the noodles to the bowl, give them a quick dunk back in boiling water, then put them straight into the bowl of soup.

3. Once your noodles hit the bowl, a countdown begins. Your goal is to finish slurping down the noodles before they become soggy and inedible. (Unless you really like soggy noodles, for some reason. We won't judge you.)

# TOOLS FOR MAKING AND EATING RAMEN

Having the right tools for making ramen is just as important as gathering your ingredients. You may find you already have the majority of these lying around your kitchen. With just a few specialty items, you can seriously level up your skills, making cooking (and eating) ramen a breeze.

## ESSENTIAL TOOLS

**Bowls:** We like to serve our ramen in deep, wide bowls that can hold at least 2 cups of liquid with plenty of room for noodles and toppings (and mixing everything up as needed). This is generally a bit bigger than most of the soup or cereal bowls you probably have in your kitchen. A wide bowl allows more space to arrange your toppings and achieve an ideal visual presentation.

**Chopsticks:** Traditional wooden chopsticks are useful both for eating ramen and for cooking; they are especially useful for agitating boiling noodles to prevent them from sticking.

**Kitchen Scale:** We have listed the recipes in this book using conventional American volume measurements, but for noodle making, specifically, you'll need a kitchen scale for accurate measurements.

**Knives:** While traditional Japanese cooks use a variety of specialty knives, you can use whatever style of knives you prefer for these recipes. They just need to be sharp.

**Ladles:** A large, 2-cup ladle is great for portioning broth. A smaller, tablespoon-size ladle is ideal for portioning oil and tare.

**Noodle Basket:** Ramen cooks use stainless-steel blanching baskets to cook noodle portions in boiling water; this way they don't have to fish the noodles out of the pot when they're done. These baskets are deeper than an ordinary mesh strainer and designed specifically for cooking fresh noodles.

**Pots and Pans:** To make broths, it's best if you have a large stockpot that is at least 12 quarts so that you have plenty of room to cook all your ingredients without anything

boiling over. You can use a wok or a high-quality skillet to fry up toppings, infuse oils, and prepare side dishes.

**Ramen Spoons:** A *chirirenge* spoon—the kind with a large, relatively flat bowl, ideally with an indentation that can hook onto the side of a bowl—is the best way to sip ramen broth. Regular spoons tend to be just a little bit too shallow. A chirirenge can provide you with adequate spoon room.

## ADDITIONAL TOOLS

**Blender/Immersion Blender:** Sometimes you'll want to strain the vegetables out of your broth. Other times you'll want to blend them in to thicken the broth's texture and intensify its flavors. An immersion blender is the best tool for blending soups, but standing blenders will work well, too. (If you use a regular blender for broths, make sure to open the valve in the lid, and cover it with a dishcloth, so that the heat from the soup won't build up and push the lid off, sending hot liquid all over your kitchen.)

**Pasta Maker with Spaghetti Attachment:** This tool is extremely helpful for making ramen noodles. Without it, the process becomes far more time and labor intensive. Ramen noodles were originally made with a hand-pulling technique—one that is rather difficult to learn, and that we wouldn't recommend for the average home cook. With a pasta maker, we can knead our dough efficiently and even use the spaghetti attachment to achieve perfectly symmetrical noodles.

**Slow Cooker and/or Instant Pot:** A slow cooker helps you simmer broths over many hours to get the maximum glutamates and flavors in the vegetable stocks. If you have an Instant Pot, you can use it as a slow cooker or use the pressure cooker settings to cook your broths in a fraction of the time.

**Spice Grinder:** While you can make all the recipes in this book with pre-ground spices, you may find your cooking subtly elevated if you take a little extra time and grind them yourself. Freshly ground spices are brighter and more flavorful, and they add an extra boost to a bowl of ramen.

# ABOUT THE RECIPES

With the story of ramen's history fresh in our minds, and a pantry fully equipped with tools and ingredients, we can begin our dive into the world of vegan ramen.

The recipes in this book will lay the groundwork for anyone to create great vegan ramen at home. First, we'll examine ramen's five essential components: oil, tare, broth, noodles, and toppings. By examining each component on its own—then understanding how to make them work together—you can level up your ramen-making skills to match the greats.

With our components ready, we now have the pieces of our puzzle laid out and ready to assemble. We'll combine these ingredients in a number of different ways to make a wide variety of different styles of ramen—from veganized classics to interpretations of local specialties.

We've done our best to curate a genuinely diverse set of recipes. Aside from our conventional shio, shoyu, miso, and tonkotsu varieties, we'll cook tsukemen and maze-men, ramen recipes that do not use broth. We'll also make ramen inspired by Persian and Korean cuisines. And we've even included a recipe developed for our own ramen food cart. Ramen is endlessly versatile, and this book will offer a deep dive into its many possibilities.

*Tsukemen (Dipping Ramen), page 73*

# CHAPTER 2
# THE ELEMENTS OF RAMEN

Broth, tare, oil, noodles, and toppings—each serves a unique purpose in the construction of a bowl of ramen. You will need all five (with some notable exceptions) to prepare the perfect bowl. As we explore each component in depth, you will find that everything pieces together quite naturally.

# BROTH

——

Traditional ramen uses a variety of animal-based soup stocks. Chicken stock and pork stock are common, as is Japan's ubiquitous dashi stock, which usually includes fish (bonito) flakes.

Fortunately, there is also a classic plant-based ramen stock that can be used without any changes: kombu dashi. This stock is made from a type of dried seaweed called kombu. Kombu contains a uniquely high concentration of glutamates—amino acids that make food taste savory and rich. Those glutamates are extracted into water through soaking and simmering, and give your liquid base a depth of flavor that goes far beyond simple saltiness.

Dried shiitake mushrooms also contain a high concentration of glutamates, and they are often used alongside the kombu in dashi. Their distinct, earthy flavor tends to cook off a bit when they're simmered, but using several different umami sources in one broth has a cumulative effect and strengthens its overall flavor.

Most ramen broths also have some fishy and smoky flavors. A third popular source of glutamates, bonito flakes, are shavings from a fermented fish product called *katsuobushi*. In vegan broths, we can add this smokiness with a dash of liquid smoke.

There are many other ways to make vegan stock for ramen. For some broths, we use the high glutamate content of oft-overlooked produce such as cabbage, tomatoes, and onion (another classic umami bomb). Much of the "meaty" quality you might expect to find in traditional ramen broths also isn't beyond our reach as vegan cooks. The plant-based glutamates from kombu, mushrooms, cabbage, and so on can easily ramp up the umami of our bowls, especially when the components are layered. Meat's other complex flavor qualities—its smokiness, acidity, or pungency—can also be synthesized with plants. Chicken stock, for instance, can be veganized simply by using the same spices and herbs used in the animal-based variety (see our Vegan "Chicken" Stock on page 25 for more details).

## VEGAN BROTH ESSENTIALS

**Mushroom Powder:** This product (which doesn't actually have a mushroom taste but adds a punch of pure umami to dishes) is commonly sold at Asian grocery stores. It is also sometimes called "mushroom broth powder" and marketed as an MSG replacement.

**Thickeners:** When cooking non-vegan ramen, cooks have access to the gelatin contained in animal products. There are several ingredients you can use to similarly thicken and enrich your soup stock.

- Agar powder (or "agar agar"): This derivative of seaweed creates a gelatinous texture when combined with liquid. It is commonly used in desserts to achieve a pudding-like texture. A small amount of agar powder can add a subtle thickness to clear soups.
- Potatoes: A single small, waxy potato (such as a fingerling, red bliss, or new potato), peeled, rinsed, and diced finely, will melt into soup stock and thicken it without adding a strong potato flavor.
- Coconut cream: Coconut cream provides creaminess to soup stock, and when it's cooked for long enough, the coconut flavor becomes milder and less noticeable.

**Vegetable Soup Stock:** Because ramen's deeper, more distinctive flavors come from the soup's tare, premade vegan stock can be a perfectly acceptable alternative to homemade stocks. You may lose some complexity, but for busy home cooks this option can save valuable prep time.

**Storage Note:** If you're not using it right away, you can freeze soup stock for up to 2 months. One technique that can help you store a lot of stock at once is to cook stock down until the flavors are highly concentrated, then pour it into ice cube trays to freeze. When you're ready to use your stock, simply pop out as many frozen stock cubes as desired and add water as needed.

# KOMBU DASHI

*Makes:* **8 cups (2 quarts)**     *Prep time:* **Overnight, for soaking**     *Cook time:* **45 minutes**

Kombu dashi is a well-established and naturally vegan ramen stock, and its natural savoriness and subtle ocean flavor make it an absolute staple. The ramen recipes in this book often mix and match kombu dashi with other, stronger stocks to temper its more intense flavors and provide balance. Note: This stock cannot be hurried along in a pressure cooker; the ingredients must be cooked with gentle care to achieve the flavor necessary for a bowl of ramen.

**1 sheet dried kombu**

**9 cups cold or room-temperature water**

1. Put the kombu into an empty sealable container, then fill the container with the water and close it. Store it overnight in the refrigerator.

2. Pour the contents of the jar into a large stockpot and place it over medium heat until it reaches a gentle simmer. Lower the heat to the lowest setting and simmer the stock for 30 minutes.

3. Remove the kombu and discard it before using the stock.

# Vegan "Chicken" Stock

*Makes:* **8 cups (2 quarts)**     *Prep time:* **15 minutes**     *Cook time:* **1 hour, 30 minutes**

The flavor of classic chicken soup comes largely from the seasoning blend rather than from the bird itself. Here we use spices like thyme, sage, and celery seed to arrive at a similar flavor. Agar powder lends a textural depth that other vegan recipes sometimes lack.

2 tablespoons (1 ounce)
  agar powder
1 cup ice-cold water
4 stalks celery, diced
2 large carrots, diced
2 yellow onions, diced
2 tablespoons canola oil
Sea salt
3 quarts (12 cups) cold or
  room-temperature water
1 teaspoon dried thyme
2 teaspoons ground
  dried sage
1 teaspoon celery seed
1 teaspoon freshly ground
  black pepper

1.  Prepare your agar powder mixture: In a small bowl, mix the agar powder with 1 cup of ice-cold water. Let it rest in the refrigerator for at least 1 hour while you prepare and cook the vegetables.

2.  In a large stockpot over medium heat, cook the celery, carrot, onion, and oil, stirring occasionally, for 20 minutes, or until soft.

3.  Add salt to taste, and once the vegetables release their natural juices (2 to 5 minutes), add the water.

4.  Bring the liquid to a simmer, then cover the pot, lower the heat to medium to maintain a low simmer, and cook the broth for 30 minutes, stirring occasionally.

5.  Add the thyme, sage, and celery seed to the pot, then add the thickened agar directly from the refrigerator. Continue simmering the stock for 30 additional minutes, until the stock has reduced by about a third from its original volume, the vegetables are translucent, and the liquid has subtly thickened. Stir in the black pepper. Strain the vegetables from the broth before using.

PRESSURE COOKER OPTION: Put the vegetables, oil and salt in the pressure cooker. Set the pressure to high and the time to 10 minutes. When cooking is complete, vent the pressure naturally, then remove the lid and add the prepared water and agar mixture. Transfer the broth to a stockpot and simmer for 30 minutes.

# CARAMELIZED CABBAGE STOCK

*Makes:* **8 cups (2 quarts)**     *Prep time:* **15 minutes**     *Cook time:* **2 hours, 30 minutes**

Caramelizing cabbage is one of our favorite food hacks, and we don't think it should be kept a secret. By cooking chopped cabbage slowly in oil for a long period of time, you can release its hidden glutamates (amino acids) and unlock the umami within. This is not unlike the more famous process of caramelizing onions. When the cooked cabbage is combined with rich coconut cream, it becomes a decadent base for building your ramen bowl.

⅛ cup canola oil

1 large head green cabbage, cored and thinly sliced

3 tablespoons sea salt

2 tablespoons mushroom powder

2 tablespoons coconut sugar

1 teaspoon turmeric

2 quarts (8 cups) cold or room-temperature water, divided

32 ounces canned coconut cream

4 medium scallions, white parts only, coarsely chopped

2 teaspoons freshly ground black pepper

1 teaspoon ground white pepper

1. Pour the oil into the bottom of a large stockpot over low heat. Once it is hot, add the cabbage in increments (roughly 1 cup at a time) and cook it on medium-high heat, stirring frequently, for 15 to 20 minutes, until the cabbage begins to brown and lose volume. At this point, add another portion of cabbage and cook, stirring frequently, until its sugar begins to release and the cabbage begins to brown. Continue this process, adding the cabbage in increments. (Adding the cabbage all at once causes it to steam, which keeps it from browning.) Once all the cabbage is added, reduce the heat to low and continue to cook for 20 minutes, or until well caramelized. Stir the cabbage occasionally while it cooks, scraping any charred bits off the bottom of the pot with a wooden spatula.

2. In a large bowl, dissolve the salt, mushroom powder, coconut sugar, and turmeric into 1 quart of water, then add the coconut cream. Add the mixture gradually to the caramelized cabbage. Increase the heat to high until the liquid is at a simmer, then reduce to medium-low heat.

3. Add the remaining 1 quart of water and the scallion, black pepper, and white pepper to the pot. Cook at a gentle simmer for 1 hour, until the liquid has reduced to about 8 cups. The broth should be a creamy golden color, and any coconut flavor should be gone.

4. Strain the vegetables from the broth before using.

PRESSURE COOKER OPTION: Put the cabbage, oil, and salt in the pressure cooker. Set the pressure to high and the time for 15 minutes. When cooking is complete, vent the pressure naturally, then transfer the cabbage to a stockpot and proceed with the recipe from step 2.

TIP: Coconut cream is often found in 32-ounce cartons or 16-ounce cans. Either cartons or cans work for this recipe. Be sure the product you buy contains a lot of saturated fat. "Coconut milk" is also sold as a milk replacement beverage with little to no fat content. That creamy, fatty quality is what you really want here.

# Vegan Demiglace

*Makes:* **12 cups (3 quarts)**   *Prep time:* **15 minutes, plus 1 hour to soak**   *Cook time:* **2 hours, 45 minutes**

Demiglace is a rich, thick soup stock used in French cuisine. This vegan version is perfect for heavier, heartier ramen bowls. We use the classic mirepoix combination of onion, celery, and carrot for flavor; tomatoes to add glutamates; and lentils and potatoes to thicken everything. Red wine adds a tangy, sweet complexity to the stock, and a single bay leaf goes a long way.

7 quarts (28 cups) cold
   or room-temperature
   water, divided
1 large russet potato,
   peeled and diced
⅓ cup canola oil
4 large white onions, diced
2 carrots, diced
2 stalks celery, diced
3 beefsteak tomatoes,
   quartered
2 tablespoons sea salt
2 teaspoons freshly
   ground black pepper
1 cup dry red wine
1 bay leaf
½ cup red lentils, rinsed
   and soaked in room-
   temperature water
   for 1 hour

1. In a medium pot, bring 1 quart (4 cups) of water to a boil. Add the potato and boil for about 30 minutes or until soft. Drain the potato and set it aside until you're ready to add it to the stock.

2. In a large stockpot over medium heat, heat the oil. Once it's hot, add the onion and cook, stirring occasionally, for about 45 minutes, or until the onion is golden brown and meltingly tender. Add the carrot, celery, and tomato, and season with the salt and pepper. Cook the vegetables, stirring occasionally, for 5 minutes, or until they begin to release their natural liquid.

3. Add the wine to the pot and scrape any brown bits off the bottom of the pot with a wooden spatula. Add the remaining 6 quarts of water to the pot, followed by the bay leaf. Add the lentils and potato to the pot.

4. Reduce the heat to medium-low and simmer the stock, uncovered, for about 1 hour, until the water reduces by half and the stock thickens. The lentils and potatoes should lose their texture and dissolve completely into the stock.

5. Using an immersion blender, puree the soup until it is smooth and glossy. The stock should have a gravy-like consistency; if it is too thick, add water and blend to your desired consistency.

PRESSURE COOKER OPTION: Put the potato, onions, celery, carrot, tomatoes, and oil in the pressure cooker. Set the pressure to high and the time for 15 minutes. Once the cooking is complete, vent the pressure naturally, then transfer the broth to a stockpot and proceed with the recipe from step 3.

TIP: If you don't own an immersion blender, you can process the soup in a regular blender in batches. If you do it this way, we recommend waiting for the stock to fully cool first, otherwise the heat may explode out of the appliance while it's blending.

# TARE

Tare doesn't have a perfect analogue in Western cooking. The word *tare*, which roughly translates to "sauce," is the foundation of a bowl of ramen. It is a concentrated combination of savory elements, and it ranges in texture from a thin liquid to a thick paste. It is usually layered into the bottom of the bowl before the broth is added. When combined with a good broth, tare gives the soup a delicious, layered richness. This exceptional savoriness is one of ramen's signature qualities.

You will often see ramen divided into three categories: shoyu, shio, and miso. This refers to the type of tare added to the bowl. (See Types of Ramen, page 7.)

Shoyu is soy sauce, the source of the salty, umami flavor associated with East and Southeast Asian cooking. A shoyu tare uses soy sauce as the primary ingredient, but it can also include any number of other flavorings, such as vinegar, sugar, spices, and so on. (Note that soy sauce is traditionally made with wheat; you can use tamari for a gluten-free alternative.)

Shio means "salt" in Japanese. Ramen made with a shio tare is light and delicately flavored, as the broth is simply enhanced with salt. Making a shio tare, however, is not as simple as adding salt to the bottom of your bowl. A shio tare is often used as a canvas to host other, stronger flavors: simmered kelp and mushrooms, rice vinegar, mirin, sugar, citrus, and sometimes even soy sauce can all be included in a shio tare.

Miso refers to soybeans fermented using salt and *koji* (a type of rice mold) to produce a thick paste with a flavor that adds a uniquely tangy punch to Japanese cooking. The type of miso you use in your ramen tare heavily impacts the flavor. Adding spices such as ground white pepper, citrus zest, and grated garlic to your miso tare will add even more dimension to the flavor.

Outside of these big three, there are many more ways to make tare. You can grind peanuts or sesame seeds into a paste for a savory and nutty tare. You can utilize European cooking techniques to create a mirepoix or soffritto of assorted aromatic vegetables. However you do it, this component of ramen is surprisingly easy to make vegan, with few to no substitutions.

## VEGAN TARE ESSENTIALS

The ingredients needed to make tare are primarily common refrigerator and pantry staples—especially in vegan kitchens, since they are essential sources of plant-based umami. A little soy sauce and miso go a long way. That said, you should consider investing in some less-common ingredients to enrich your tare. Dark soy sauce, sake, mirin, rice vinegar, chili paste, and toasted sesame oil all add wonderful flavors to ramen.

The key to creating a tare is to identify your primary flavor and then layer other ingredients on top. A balanced tare has salty, sweet, acidic, aromatic, and umami flavors. You can bring these ingredients together in the bottom of your bowl just before the broth and noodles are ready, or you can premix them and store them in the refrigerator. (Tare can be made up to a week in advance.)

# SHOYU TARE

*Makes: **1 cup** / Serves: **16***      *Prep time: **10 minutes***

This umami-bomb tare uses dark soy sauce for its color and salty richness, and light soy sauce to balance out some of the dark's intensity. Rice vinegar and mirin add acidity; light brown sugar rounds out the flavor with a touch of sweetness, while garlic and ginger both add an aromatic punch.

¾ cup Kombu Dashi
(page 24)

2 tablespoons light
soy sauce

1 tablespoon dark
soy sauce

1 tablespoon mirin

1 teaspoon rice vinegar

1 teaspoon grated garlic

1 teaspoon grated ginger

1 teaspoon brown sugar

1. In a small bowl, whisk together the dashi, light and dark soy sauces, mirin, rice vinegar, garlic, ginger, and sugar until the sugar has dissolved.

2. Ladle 2 tablespoons of the mixture directly into each ramen bowl, or store it in an airtight container in the refrigerator for up to 1 week.

# Shio Citrus Tare

*Makes: **1 cup** / Serves: **16***     *Prep time: **10 minutes***

Our shio tare of choice is light and has refreshing citrus notes. Combining salt and acid heightens the complexity of your ramen bowl and elevates the flavors of the broth. We're lucky enough to have access to yuzu, a Japanese citrus fruit with a distinctive, fragrant flavor. If you cannot obtain yuzu, use a Meyer lemon or a 50/50 split of freshly squeezed lime and orange juice.

**1 tablespoon sea salt**

**1 teaspoon grated citrus zest**

**½ teaspoon granu- lated sugar**

**¾ cup Kombu Dashi (page 24)**

**3 tablespoons freshly squeezed citrus juice**

**1 tablespoon mirin**

1. In a small bowl, combine the salt, citrus zest, and sugar. Gently whisk the ingredients to extract the oils from the zest. Add the dashi, citrus juice, and mirin, and whisk until combined.

2. Ladle 2 tablespoons of the mixture directly into each ramen bowl, or store it in an airtight container in the refrigerator for up to 1 week.

# Spicy Miso Tare

*Makes:* **1 cup** / *Serves:* **16**     *Prep time:* **5 minutes**

This dense, flavorful tare is perfect for richly flavored ramen such as tonkotsu. Our central ingredient here is doubanjiang, a spicy Chinese bean sauce. This paste is usually made from fermented chilis, soybeans, and broad beans. We use it in much the same way that we use miso in our other tare recipes.

½ cup miso paste

¼ cup doubanjiang

2 tablespoons toasted
  sesame oil

2 tablespoons mirin

2 teaspoons rice vinegar

2 teaspoons granulated
  sugar

1. In a small bowl, combine the miso paste, doubanjiang, sesame oil, mirin, rice vinegar, and sugar. Mix everything until you have a uniform paste.

2. Ladle 2 tablespoons of the mixture directly into each ramen bowl, or store it in an airtight container in the refrigerator for up to 1 week.

# Soffritto Tare

*Makes: ¾ cup / Serves: 14*      *Prep time: 10 minutes*      *Cook time: 1 hour, 10 minutes*

This American-style tare (which uses a French-style mirepoix of onion, carrot, and celery), was inspired by Ivan Orkin, who may be our favorite American ramen chef. At his restaurant, Ivan Ramen, Orkin uses aspects of his Jewish upbringing to inform the way he makes his ramen. Think of this tare as a vegan chicken stock with some mild Japanese elements, like mirin and sake, to help it fit it into the ramen mold.

2 tablespoons canola oil
1 cup finely diced onion
½ cup finely diced carrot
½ cup finely diced celery
1 garlic clove, minced (optional)
1 tablespoon sake
1 tablespoon mirin
1 tablespoon soy sauce
Sea salt

1. Pour the oil into a sauté pan on medium-low heat. Once hot, add the onion and gently sauté for 20 minutes, or until the onion softens. Add the carrot and celery and sauté for 20 minutes, until soft.

2. Increase the heat to medium-high and cook, stirring frequently, until the vegetables begin to brown, about 10 minutes. If using the garlic, add it now and cook everything for 1 minute more.

3. Add the sake, mirin, and soy sauce, and scrape the brown bits from the bottom of the pan with a wooden spatula. Reduce the heat to low, and let the sauce come to a simmer and cook for 10 minutes. Season to taste with salt.

4. Ladle 2 tablespoons of the mixture directly into each ramen bowl, or store it in an airtight container in the refrigerator for up to 1 week.

# OIL AND FAT

Fat is a ramen chef's secret weapon, unlocking the full flavor potential of every dish. Fats imbue ramen noodles with a tactile slipperiness. They also create a stunning visual effect as droplets of oil decorate the surface of the broth. Finally, fat is a conduit that allows ramen's other components to overlap elegantly, helping blend flavors and aromas.

In conventional ramen broths that use animal products, there is often some amount of fat in the broth itself, even before the addition of an infused oil. This fat is sometimes rendered out of the meat to be augmented and then re-added later, in a controlled volume. Vegan ramen broths, however, tend to have lower fat contents.

Regardless of what type of broth you use, a bowl of ramen is elevated immensely by adding a ladleful of aromatic oil, which can be either mixed in with the tare at the bottom of the bowl or added to the surface of the broth.

Another trendy ramen topping in Japan is butter. Luckily, American vegans have come a long way since margarine, and we have access to a variety of lacto-fermented vegan butter products we can use.

Because fat rises and pools on the surface of the broth, the oil in your soup is the first thing that will hit both your nose and mouth when you take a sip, so it's important to infuse it with maximally pleasing flavors and aromas. Many of these oils were traditionally infused with garlic, shallot, or scallions, but nowadays, chefs also use a variety of other ingredients, such as chilis, spices, or fresh herbs.

While flavored oils can occasionally be found at the grocery store, nothing can match the intensity of a freshly infused batch. The process is a bit time-consuming, but it's simple enough, and this one small step will elevate your home-cooked ramen to a professional level.

## OIL AND FAT ESSENTIALS

When making your own flavor-infused oils, start with a neutral-flavored oil, such as canola or sunflower oil. ("Vegetable oil" is often simply soybean oil renamed to avoid a strange stigma around soy.)

Avoid flavorful oils, such as extra-virgin olive oil or *unrefined* coconut oil. Their naturally strong flavors muddle the end result. Refined coconut oil (in contrast to virgin coconut oil) has a much milder flavor. It also has a high saturated fat content, which can create a butter-like texture in your bowl.

Feel free to experiment with any varieties of oil you have at home—just be mindful of the oil's cooking temperature and your desired flavor outcome.

Once you have selected an oil, you can choose the ingredients you want to use in the infusion. What you infuse your oil with will determine how long its shelf life is and the method of infusion: Ingredients containing water, such as garlic or shallot, will necessitate a "low and slow" infusion. These typically do not have a long shelf life—only a few days at most. Dry ingredients, such as chili flakes, herbs, and spices, can be either cold-infused or flash-infused (this is done by pouring hot oil onto them).

# INFUSED GARLIC OIL

*Makes: **1¼ cups** / Serves: **11***     *Prep time: **5 minutes, plus***     *Cook time: **20 minutes***
*30 minutes for cooling*

By slowly cooking fresh garlic in an unflavored oil (such as canola) at a low temperature, we can draw out the alium's pungent aromatics. This is more useful than adding the garlic directly to ramen broth, because when cooked for long periods in liquid, garlic's flavor tends to dissipate quickly. Infusing garlic in oil ensures you'll never lose the full flavor and aroma of this amazing plant.

**2 heads garlic**
**1½ cups canola oil**

1. Peel the garlic cloves and crush them with the flat side of a knife or the back of a wooden spoon.

2. In a small saucepan over medium-low heat, gently warm the oil. The oil should come to a very low simmer, about 160°F. Add the garlic cloves and let them cook for 10 for 20 minutes, stirring occasionally. (Higher heat increases the risk of burning the garlic, but anything lower than 160°F makes for a very weak infusion.)

3. When the oil is intensely aromatic and the garlic has softened, remove the pot from the heat and allow the oil to cool completely. Strain the oil into an airtight glass container, discarding the garlic, and refrigerate it for no more than 4 days. Use 2 tablespoons of the oil in each ramen bowl.

COOKING TIP: You can increase or reduce the garlic in this recipe, according to your flavor preference and the size of your garlic cloves. You can also turn the heat to medium to get a slightly deeper flavor in the oil, but avoid getting too much color on the garlic as it cooks, or it might burn.

# Infused Scallion Oil

*Makes: 1¼ cups / Serves: 11*   *Prep time: 5 minutes, plus*   *Cook time: 30 minutes*
                                                   *30 minutes for cooling*

Our infused scallion oil uses refined coconut oil to achieve a solid texture when chilled. The saturated fat from the coconut oil will imbue the oil with a buttery texture to accompany the fresh scallion flavor.

**1½ cups refined coconut oil**

**6 to 10 scallions, white and light green parts only, cut into 1-inch segments (reserve the dark green parts for topping your ramen)**

**1 medium shallot, coarsely chopped**

1. In a small saucepan over low heat, melt the coconut oil. When the oil has liquified and is just below a gentle simmer (about 160°F), add the scallion and shallot. Cook until the scallions and shallot are golden in color, 20 to 30 minutes, stirring occasionally. (Do not raise the temperature at any point during the cooking process. Keep it just below a gentle simmer or about 160°F.)

2. Remove the saucepan from the heat and carefully strain the oil into a heatproof container, discarding the scallions and shallot. Allow the oil to cool completely, then seal it in an airtight container and refrigerate it for no more than 4 days. Use 2 tablespoons of the oil in each ramen bowl.

COOKING TIP: Since coconut oil has a low smoke point, it is important to cook it at a low heat to avoid decomposition. You can also use refined coconut oil to make garlic oil or any type of hot oil infusion.

# INFUSED CHILI OIL

*Makes: **1½ cups** / Serves: **11***      *Prep time: **1 minute***      *Cook time: **5 minutes***

There are a huge variety of chili flakes available—as many types of flakes as there are peppers. We're not just talking about the packets of crushed red peppers you might sprinkle on a slice of pizza; from chipotle peppers to Thai peppers, the choices are endless. Pouring hot oil over dry chili flakes is a technique that originated in China. The resulting oil produces a spicy punch of flavor that will send your bowl over the top.

**⅔ cup chili flakes (such as Thai chili flakes or Sichuan chili flakes)**

**1½ cups canola oil or Infused Garlic Oil (page 38)**

1. Put the chili flakes into a heat-safe, airtight container (metal or ceramic will work). Mix a few drops of cold water into the flakes so they are slightly damp.

2. In a small saucepan over medium heat, heat the oil until small bubbles form; do not allow it to boil. (If using a thermometer, bring the oil to 250°F to 270°F, never above 350°F.)

3. When the oil is hot, quickly and carefully pour it over the chili flakes. The flakes should sizzle for a minute, then settle. Allow the oil to cool completely, then seal the container and store the oil in the refrigerator for no more than 4 days. Use 2 tablespoons of the oil in each ramen bowl.

# Cold-Infused Rosemary Oil

*Makes: **1½ cups** / Serves: **12***        *Prep time: **2 weeks***

Certain oils can be infused without any heat, which extends their shelf life. Unlike hot-infused oil, any oil can be used in a cold infusion—even olive oil. Try to use an oil that stays liquid when chilled—basically anything other than coconut oil, vegan butter, or Crisco. Herbs, like the rosemary used in this recipe, have a powerful aromatic quality that stands out and complements many ramen bowls.

**3 sprigs rosemary**

**1½ cups oil of your choice**

1.  Wash the rosemary sprigs and pat them dry, then allow them to air dry for up to 24 hours so that no moisture is left on the leaves.

2.  Pour your oil into an airtight glass pint jar and add the rosemary. Seal the container and store the oil in the refrigerator to infuse. The flavor will develop and deepen over time, so you'll want to wait at least 2 weeks to use the oil, but the longer you leave it, the stronger the flavor will get. The oil keeps indefinitely, as long as it is refrigerated and kept clean. Use 2 tablespoons of the oil in each ramen bowl.

SUBSTITUTION TIP: Try thyme, lavender, or sage in place of the rosemary.

Chili Oil

Shio Citrus Tare

Caramelized
Cabbage Stock

Garlic Oil

Vegan
Chicken
Stock

*Kombu Dashi
Broth Base*

*Spicy
Miso
Tare*

*Vegan
Demiglace*

*Shoyu Tare*

# NOODLES

What is it about ramen noodles that makes them so uniquely tasty? It's no secret that the world loves carbohydrates, whether it's potatoes, rice, bread, or pasta; we just can't get enough of these essential starches. What sets ramen noodles apart from other types of pasta is one simple addition—an ingredient called *kansui*.

Kansui is an alkaline solution of water, sodium bicarbonate, and potassium carbonate. It imbues ramen noodles with their signature color and springy texture. If you've ever wondered how instant ramen noodles maintain their curly shape after boiling, you can thank the kansui.

Here we will provide a breakdown of how to shop for ramen noodles, look at gluten-free options, and offer a recipe for making your own noodles at home.

## STORE-BOUGHT NOODLES

Premade, fresh ramen noodles can be found in the frozen and refrigerated sections of Asian grocery stores. Look for noodles with a simple ingredients list that includes flour, water, salt, and kansui. Some noodles may have other types of flour mixed in for taste and texture, such as barley or buckwheat. Some will indicate they are "processed with alkali," which refers to the addition of kansui. When kansui is present, the alkaline components are clearly listed in the ingredients. Any noodle that does not list an alkaline component is probably not the noodle you're looking for.

Our food cart uses noodles made by Umi Organic; their noodles are currently available in stores across the West Coast. Another popular, high-quality brand is Sun Noodle; they are sold across the United States. (Some fresh noodle recipes use egg, so if you're buying fresh or frozen ramen noodles, be sure to check the ingredients list.)

If you are cooking gluten-free, there are a variety of noodle options available to suit different tastes. One popular ramen substitute is soba, a traditional Japanese noodle made of buckwheat. Look for soba noodles that use only buckwheat; most soba noodle manufacturers also use some wheat in their noodles, so it's important to look carefully at the ingredients list. Eden Foods makes a 100 percent buckwheat soba product that can be found in many organic grocery stores.

Lotus Foods makes several good gluten-free dried noodle options with a variety of alternative flours. You could consider rice noodles as well; they are a staple of Southeast Asian cuisine. Lastly, you could try shirataki noodles, a chewy, slightly rubbery type made from konjac root; they're especially popular with people who have stricter dietary restrictions.

## HOMEMADE NOODLES

Making ramen noodles at home might be a somewhat time- and labor-intensive process, but it's not actually that difficult. All that goes into them are a few simple ingredients: flour, water, salt, and kansui. (And since this is all they have in them, homemade noodles are vegan by default.)

As you'll see from the list above, the only unusual ingredient needed for this process is the kansui. You can purchase a premade kansui solution in some Asian grocery stores, but it is uncommon enough that you might have to order it online. You can also make a DIY version of kansui at home using heat-treated baking soda (see page 47).

# TRADITIONAL RAMEN NOODLES

*Serves:* **8**          *Prep time:* **1 hour, 30 minutes**          *Cook time:* **2 minutes**

You're ready to take your bowls to the next level and make your own ramen noodles from scratch! While the ingredients for ramen noodles are simple, making them requires techniques that can take some time to learn. Our recipe here is a great place to start, but you may find that it takes a few attempts to get it right. Noodle makers practice for years before they're able to reach a level of mastery. Having a pasta maker (the kind usually used for Italian pastas like spaghetti) simplifies parts of the process. For enthusiastic vegan ramen heads, we recommend starting with some fresh store-bought noodles and focusing on mastering the other four components first. Then, when you're ready, dust your hands with flour and get ready to try your hand at noodles.

2 teaspoons (8 grams) kansui, store-bought or homemade (page 47)
2 teaspoons (8 grams) sea salt
1 cup ice-cold water
2¼ cups bread flour
Cornstarch, for dusting

1. In a small bowl, mix the kansui and salt into the ice-cold water. Put the flour into a large mixing bowl, then pour the kansui mixture in slowly, mixing vigorously as you go. "Crumbles" will begin to appear. (Because this is a low-hydration dough, it won't come together naturally.)

2. Transfer the dough crumbles into a resealable plastic bag, close the bag, and let the dough rest for 45 minutes.

3. Without removing the crumbles from the bag, knead them until they become a cohesive mass, then transfer the dough to a clean work surface dusted with cornstarch.

4. Use a rolling pin dusted with cornstarch to roll the dough out into a 4-inch-wide sheet. (Use more cornstarch as needed to prevent sticking.) Begin rolling the sheet through your pasta machine on the widest (likely 4-inch) setting. After the first pass through the machine, fold the sheet in half, then roll it through the pasta machine again at the same setting. Repeat this process at least two times, until the sheet is glossy and smooth.

5.  Change the pasta machine setting to the next, slightly narrower setting and roll the dough through. Repeat this process, making the setting narrower each time, until the dough is able to pass through the fourth-widest setting without any resistance (the dough will be about ⅛-inch thick).

6.  Dust the noodle sheet generously with cornstarch. Fit the spaghetti attachment to the pasta maker and feed the sheet through, to cut it into long noodles. Dust the noodles with more cornstarch, and fluff them a bit to keep them from sticking.

7.  Seal the noodles in a glass storage container and refrigerate them overnight so that the gluten can relax. Use one-eighth of the noodles for each bowl of ramen.

# HOMEMADE KANSUI

Preheat the oven to 275°F. Line a baking sheet with aluminum foil. Sprinkle 2 cups of baking soda onto the foil, spreading it evenly. Bake until the weight of the baking soda has reduced by one-third. This should take roughly 1 hour, 15 minutes. Cool the baked baking soda, and store it in an airtight container. This makes about 1⅓ cups and is enough kansui to make more than a dozen batches of ramen noodles. (That's more than enough to try every single ramen recipe in this book!)

# TOPPINGS

There is more to ramen toppings than the typical slice of char-siu and a soft-boiled egg. There are classics, and then there are toppings that are unconventional, experimental, and downright controversial. No matter what you use, it's still a bowl of ramen.

You'll often see scallions (negi), bamboo shoots (menma), mushrooms (shiitake), seaweed (nori), bean sprouts (moyashi), cabbage (kyabetsu), corn (kon), and butter (bataa) on traditional bowls of ramen. These staples often require little preparation. Scallions are sliced thin and sprinkled on top as a garnish, sheets of nori are placed along the side of the bowl just before serving, and mushrooms don't need much more than a light stir-fry (see page 49). Some toppings, like bamboo shoots or bean sprouts, can go straight from their packaging into the bowl.

Notice how most of these toppings are plants? Because ramen broth is traditionally made from animal bones, the soup itself tends to be incredibly rich, oily, and fatty. This is coupled with the salty tare and carb-heavy noodles, and the combination is so hearty that you may only get a few bites into your ramen before you start to crave something lighter. These fresh vegetables offset that richness and create a more balanced overall flavor; they also add a delightfully crunchy texture to each bite. You can experiment with your favorite vegetables in various preparations—raw, stir-fried, roasted, or pickled.

## TOPPING ESSENTIALS

When it comes to vegan ramen, there are a few traditional toppings that are difficult to duplicate. Eggs, fish cakes, and fatty char-siu have no one-to-one vegan substitute. We see this as an opportunity to think outside the bowl and create new favorites. Tofu, tempeh, seitan, mushrooms, jackfruit, and even eggplant make fantastic ramen toppings for a savory, meaty bite.

With toppings, less is often more. Two or three simply prepared toppings will round out a deeply flavorful ramen bowl. Vegetables that require only a quick chop or sauté, like scallions, white onion, cabbage, spinach, or tomato, work wonders for your bowl.

Ready-to-serve toppings like bean sprouts, bamboo shoots, corn, fried onions, and pickled red ginger (*beni shoga*) add an element of convenience for a quick and easy bowl. Toppings that require some preparation can be made in advance and simply reheated just before serving.

# Seared Mushrooms

*Serves:* **4**          *Prep time:* **5 minutes**          *Cook time:* **20 minutes**

Shiitake mushrooms are the first choice when it comes to mushroom toppings because of their subtle, nutty flavor and widespread availability. If you're lucky enough to have access to harder-to-find varieties, lion's mane mushrooms are our personal favorite. Other great options for searing are maitake and oyster varieties. Regardless of which type you pick, mushrooms are a versatile protein with a texture that can rival animal meat when prepared properly. Well-seared mushrooms may even win over your most skeptical non-vegan friends.

1 tablespoon canola oil

12 ounces fresh mushrooms (about 4 cups), wiped clean with a damp paper towel, stems removed

½ teaspoon sea salt

⅛ teaspoon ground white pepper

1 tablespoon light soy sauce

1 tablespoon mirin

1 teaspoon rice vinegar

1. In a large skillet over medium-high heat, heat the oil. Once it's hot, add the mushrooms to the skillet, arranging them so that there are no overlapping pieces. Reduce the heat to low, and let the mushrooms cook undisturbed until the bottoms begin to brown and crisp, 10 to 15 minutes.

2. Season the mushrooms lightly with salt and pepper, then cook, stirring frequently, until their liquids release, 2 to 4 minutes.

3. Add the soy sauce, mirin, and rice vinegar to the skillet. Increase the heat to high, and toss the mushrooms around the skillet to coat them evenly with the seasoning, about 1 minute. Remove the mushrooms from the heat and add them to your ramen while they're still hot or refrigerate them in an airtight container for up to 2 days.

# FRIED SWEET-GLAZE TOFU

*Serves: 4*            *Prep time: 2 minutes*            *Cook time: 20 minutes*

Tofu has an unfairly maligned reputation. There are lots of methods we can use to prepare it, and we find it absurd that this protein is still often served with little to no seasoning and cooked without regard for its culinary potential. While trendier protein alternatives become increasingly popular, we still return to tofu as the most adaptable and affordable "alternative" protein. The method we use for this particular preparation is relatively simple: We fry the tofu with a sweet soy glaze. If you're a tofu skeptic yourself, we hope this recipe will change your mind.

½ cup light soy sauce
½ cup light brown sugar
¼ cup water
2 tablespoons mirin
2 tablespoons rice vinegar
1 teaspoon onion powder
½ teaspoon ground ginger
1 (16-ounce) block
   extra-firm tofu
Cornstarch, for dusting
2 tablespoons canola oil

1.  In a small saucepan, combine the soy sauce, brown sugar, water, mirin, rice vinegar, onion powder, and ginger. Gently heat the mixture on low, stirring often, until the sugar is dissolved, then remove the saucepan from the heat and set it aside to cool.

2.  Drain the tofu of its liquid and gently press it between paper towels to remove excess moisture. Cut the tofu into ½-inch cubes. In a large bowl, dust the tofu cubes evenly with cornstarch, coating them until their outsides are dry.

3.  Heat the oil in a skillet over medium heat. Once it's hot, add the tofu pieces. Fry each side for about 2 minutes, until they are golden brown and crispy.

4.  When the pieces of tofu are thoroughly crisped on all sides, add the sauce to the skillet, and toss the tofu to coat every piece. Reduce the heat to medium-low, and allow the tofu to simmer, stirring occasionally, until the sauce has thickened, about 5 minutes. Remove the tofu from the heat. Add it to your ramen or refrigerate it in an airtight container for up to 3 days.

# Twice-Thawed and Baked Tofu

*Serves: 4*  *Prep time: 2 days*  *Cook time: 1 hour*

This is a more involved recipe, one that allows us to modify the tofu's texture to create a juicy and "meaty" quality. To do this, we freeze and then completely thaw the tofu twice before cooking it. This makes the tofu spongier and more porous, which makes it easier to squeeze out its liquid. After we freeze and thaw the tofu twice, we can replace that liquid with a savory marinade. This recipe requires you to commit to a multiday prep time, but the result is a juicy, tender protein that can put animal protein to shame.

1 (16-ounce) block
  extra-firm tofu
1 cup vegetable broth
1 tablespoon sesame oil
1 teaspoon dark soy sauce
1 teaspoon rice vinegar
1 teaspoon mirin
1 teaspoon light
  brown sugar
1 teaspoon garlic powder
1 teaspoon freshly ground
  black pepper
½ teaspoon white pepper

1. Drain the tofu of its liquid and gently press it between paper towels to remove excess moisture.

2. Place the whole block of tofu in an airtight container, and freeze it for 24 hours. Remove the tofu and thaw it completely, then drain the excess liquid once again.

3. Repeat this process, freezing and draining the tofu a second time, so that the texture of the tofu becomes dry and porous and it is able to absorb liquid easily.

4. Preheat the oven to 300°F. In an oven-safe skillet, mix together the broth, sesame oil, soy sauce, vinegar, mirin, brown sugar, garlic powder, black pepper, and white pepper. Cut the thawed tofu into even ¼-inch strips (length- or widthwise). Put the tofu strips into the skillet, making sure they are completely covered by the marinade.

5. Bake the tofu for 45 minutes to 1 hour, or until most of the marinade is absorbed. Add the strips to your ramen, or refrigerate them in an airtight container for up to 5 days.

COOKING TIP: For a crispier exterior, sear each side of the tofu in a hot, oiled skillet before slicing it and baking it in the marinade.

# GARLIC-OIL CORN

*Serves:* **4**          *Prep time:* **3 minutes**          *Cook time:* **40 minutes**

Corn is a popular ramen topping, and for good reason. It can add a sweet splash of flavor to each bite, and the yellow color pops prettily in the bowl. To make corn work for ramen, a bit of finessing is required: Plain corn may work in a pinch, but by toasting it in salt and garlic oil, you can draw out much of its innate sweetness while simultaneously adding aromatic and savory notes.

**2 cups corn kernels**

**3 tablespoons Infused Garlic Oil (page 38)**

**2 teaspoons sea salt**

1. Fill a small pot about halfway with water and bring it to a boil. Add the corn and cook it for 1 to 2 minutes, just until it softens. Drain the corn.

2. In a medium skillet over medium heat, warm the infused oil briefly. Add the corn, spreading it in an even layer. Without stirring, cook the corn until one side is nicely browned, 10 to 15 minutes. Stir in the salt to taste. Continue to cook, stirring occasionally until each kernel has taken on some light brown color, about 10 minutes. Use it in your ramen or refrigerate it in an airtight container for up to 3 days.

TIP: This recipe works best with fresh corn cut from the cob, but canned or frozen corn works fine as well.

# Seasoned Wilted Spinach

*Serves:* **4**              *Prep time:* **20 minutes**              *Cook time:* **15 minutes**

It won't make you instantly sprout biceps like Popeye, but with the right seasoning, spinach can go from a plain green to a decadent topping. By wilting the spinach and then immediately blanching it in ice water, you can make sure the leaves are tender but not mushy and retain their bright green color. Soy sauce, sesame oil, and mirin add the small, extra kick the spinach needs to turn it into something special.

**Sea salt**

**1 (12-ounce) bag prewashed spinach (about 10 cups)**

**1 teaspoon light soy sauce**

**1 teaspoon toasted sesame oil**

**½ teaspoon mirin**

**1 teaspoon toasted sesame seeds**

1. Prepare a large bowl with water and ice.

2. Bring a large pot of salted water to boil and add the spinach. Cook the spinach until just before the leaves wilt completely, about 1 minute. Drain the spinach and immediately submerge it in the ice water.

3. When the spinach has cooled, drain it again and then squeeze it to remove as much liquid as possible. Put the spinach in a small bowl and add the soy sauce, sesame oil, mirin, and sesame seeds; toss the spinach to coat the leaves evenly. Let the spinach marinate for about 10 minutes before adding it to your ramen. The spinach is best and most flavorful if used right away; if making it ahead, refrigerate it in an airtight container for 1 day.

# Soy Curl "Chicken"

*Makes: **3 cups***        *Prep time: **10 minutes***        *Cook time: **35 minutes***

Soy curls are a dried meat alternative made from soy protein. We've found them significantly easier to cook with than textured vegetable protein (TVP), another meat alternative made from the same stuff. A company called Butler produces a widely available brand of soy curls that, when marinated and cooked, as in this recipe, do a great job of imitating the taste and texture of chicken.

**2 cups Vegan "Chicken" Stock (page 25)**

**½ (8-ounce) package soy curls**

**4 tablespoons light soy sauce**

**3 tablespoons mirin**

**1 tablespoon light brown sugar**

**1 teaspoon grated garlic**

**1 teaspoon grated ginger**

**⅓ cup canola oil**

**2 teaspoons vegan chicken seasoning**

**1 tablespoon nutritional yeast**

**Toasted sesame seeds, for garnish**

1. In a large stockpot, bring the stock to a boil. Add the soy curls, turn off the heat, and allow the curls to sit for about 10 minutes, until they have absorbed most of the liquid. Drain the soy curls and squeeze out any excess moisture.

2. In a small bowl, combine the soy sauce, mirin, brown sugar, garlic, and ginger.

3. Pour the canola oil into a large pan and heat it on medium-high. Add the soy curls, vegan chicken seasoning, and nutritional yeast, and stir to combine. Cook the soy curls, stirring occasionally, until they're lightly golden brown in some places, about 10 minutes.

4. Add the sauce mixture to the skillet and stir the soy curls until they're evenly coated. Continue to cook, stirring frequently, until they look glossy, 2 to 3 minutes. Remove the curls from the heat and garnish them with toasted sesame seeds. Add the curls to your ramen while hot, or refrigerate them in an airtight container for up to 5 days.

# BUILDING AND SAVORING

Now that we've covered the basics, it's time to assemble your long-awaited bowl of ramen. This step happens quickly and requires that we have all previously mentioned components ready to use. At this point, you may boil your noodles and set them aside in a bowl of ice water to prevent overcooking. (Keep your pot of water boiling; you'll need it later!) You may also warm any toppings that have been prepared in advance.

The bottom layer of your bowl of ramen will consist of the tare and/or oil. Add these components before your broth. At this point you may also add additional seasonings that you want to mingle with the broth. The idea of this bottom layer is to establish flavors in your ramen that may have been cooked out if added directly to the broth while it's simmering. Keeping these seasonings separate accentuates their freshness and heightens their flavor profile.

Next, pour in the piping-hot broth and give it a mix. Using a mesh strainer (preferably a deep, basket-shaped one), quickly dunk the chilled noodles into that pot of still-boiling water to bring them up to temperature. Shake off the excess water, then carefully lower the noodles into your bowl of soup. Add your toppings and garnishes and enjoy!

Ramen is a time-sensitive dining experience, best enjoyed hot and fresh. This is why it is ideal to have your components ready before the assembly and serving process, especially when serving multiple people. You should start eating right away, while the soup is still steaming hot. By slurping your broth and noodles, you can cool and aerate the ramen as you go. Slurping may be jarring for Americans, but it is standard practice for ramen eaters in Japan, and we strongly encourage you to try it.

# PART TWO

# BOWLS AND SIDES

Now we arrive at our full ramen recipes. If you're itching to start cooking up some delicious vegan ramen, you're in for a treat. All the recipes in this chapter incorporate the building blocks of the component recipes in part 1, so we encourage you to look back on those recipes as needed. With a few exceptions, these ramen recipes are designed to make four servings.

While ramen already contains a lot of flavors, you may want some delicious sides to complement your bowl. The last chapter of this book includes recipes to make some popular side dishes (and delicious drinks). Having a side dish with your ramen is by no means mandatory, but with the right combination, the contrast between dishes can heighten the eating experience and round out your meal. (You may even want to use these sides as toppings in your ramen.)

The ramen and side dish recipes are inspired by many different places and traditions, ranging from classic Japanese ramens to American and global adaptations. A few are unique spins of our own, based on our cultures, our lives, and our experience as vegan chefs and food cart owners. We hope that by the time you've tried out a few of these recipes, you'll feel as confident as we do when it comes to making delicious vegan ramen at home.

*Fancy "Elevated" Instant Ramen, page 60*

# CHAPTER 3
# RAMEN

# FANCY "ELEVATED" INSTANT RAMEN

*Serves: **1***     *Prep time: **15 minutes***     *Cook time: **10 minutes***

Instant ramen noodles are a pantry staple all over the world—a quick, cheap, and convenient meal option that can keep for years. Here, we elevate this staple by adding instant ramen's "missing" components (tare, oil, and toppings). Now we can transform our humble instant ramen into a meal worth bragging about.

1 tablespoon Infused Garlic Oil (page 38)

2 teaspoon Shoyu Tare (page 32)

1 teaspoon sea salt, plus more for seasoning

4 cups water

3 leaves baby bok choy, separated

1 (8-ounce) package instant ramen noodles with seasoning packet

¼ to ⅓ cup Seared Mushrooms (page 49), made with shiitake mushrooms

1 scallion, thinly sliced crosswise

½ teaspoon shichimi togarashi or finely ground red pepper

½ teaspoon toasted sesame seeds

1. Ladle the infused oil, tare, and salt into the bottom of a serving bowl. Mix to incorporate.

2. In a medium saucepan, bring the water to a boil. Add the sliced bok choy leaves and cook them for 5 minutes, or until they begin to soften. Using tongs, remove the bok choy and transfer it to a plate. Sprinkle each leaf with a pinch of salt. Keep the water in the saucepan boiling.

3. Pour the contents of the seasoning packet into the boiling water. Put the instant ramen noodle block into the saucepan, and cook the noodles according to the package instructions (usually 2 to 4 minutes—don't overcook the noodles; they will continue to soften in the hot soup as you eat).

4. Ladle 2 cups of the boiling liquid into the bowl (you will not use all the liquid), then add the noodles. Mix everything to incorporate the tare and oil. Garnish the bowl with the bok choy, seared mushrooms, and scallion. Finish the bowl with a sprinkle of togarashi and sesame seeds.

# Simple Shio (Salt) Ramen

*Serves:* **4**          *Prep time:* **15 minutes**          *Cook time:* **20 minutes**

Standard shio ramen is often made by combining chicken broth and a salt-based tare, which come together to make a light, clear soup. You can find many variations of shio ramen, and various regions of Japan have their own versions of the dish. Here, we use a citrusy tare and Vegan "Chicken" Stock as the base for a simple salt ramen that is light on toppings but bursting with flavor. We also use furikake as a simple swap for the sheets of toasted nori that are traditionally found in this dish. (Some furikake brands contain bonito flakes or other fish products, so be sure to check the label before purchasing.)

4 tablespoons Infused
   Garlic Oil (page 38)
4 tablespoons Shio Citrus
   Tare (page 33)
6 cups Vegan "Chicken"
   Stock (page 25)
2 cups Kombu Dashi
   (page 24)
2 cups shredded
   green cabbage
1¼ pounds (3 cups or
   560g) fresh ramen
   noodles, store-bought or
   homemade (page 46),
   divided into 4 portions
3 scallions, thinly sliced
   crosswise
Nori goma furikake,
   for garnish

1. Ladle 1 tablespoon of infused garlic oil and 1 tablespoon of shio citrus tare into each bowl. Mix to incorporate.

2. In a large stockpot over medium-high heat, bring the stock and the kombu dashi to a simmer. While the stock is heating, prepare a large bowl of cold water and ice. When the broth is hot, place the cabbage in a fine-mesh strainer and lower it into the broth to cook the cabbage directly in the soup just until it softens, about 3 minutes. Immediately remove the cabbage (in the strainer) and cool it in the ice bath.

3. Fill a medium saucepan three-quarters full of water and bring it to a rolling boil over high heat. Cook each noodle portion, separately, for about 1 minute, then place it in the ice-water bath.

4. Ladle 2 cups of hot stock into each bowl and mix well. Just before serving, dunk each portion of noodles back into the boiling water, shake off any excess water, and place it in the bowl. Garnish the bowls with one-quarter of the cabbage, scallions, and furikake.

# Yuzu Shio Ramen

*Serves: 4*          *Prep time: 10 minutes*          *Cook time: 20 minutes*

This yuzu shio ramen is a vegan adaptation of the signature dish at one of Tokyo's premier ramen restaurants, Afuri. Yuzu, an iconic Japanese citrus fruit, adds a delectable tartness to the bowl. While it can be difficult to source fresh yuzu fruit, yuzu juice is more widely available, especially at Japanese markets. If neither the fruit or the juice is available, use a Meyer lemon instead for a comparable flavor.

4 tablespoons Infused Scallion Oil (page 39)

4 tablespoons Shio Citrus Tare (page 33)

4 teaspoons yuzu juice or extract

2 teaspoons yuzu zest or other citrus zest, divided

1 (14-ounce) can bamboo shoots, drained

2 teaspoons light soy sauce

6 cups Vegan "Chicken" Stock (page 25)

2 cups Kombu Dashi (page 24)

1¼ pounds (3 cups or 560g) fresh ramen noodles, store-bought or homemade (page 46), divided into 4 portions

1 block Twice-Thawed and Baked Tofu (page 51)

3 scallions, thinly sliced crosswise

1 toasted nori sheet, cut into 4 (2-by-4-inch) pieces

1. Ladle 1 tablespoon of infused scallion oil, 1 tablespoon of shio citrus tare, 1 teaspoon of yuzu juice, and ¼ teaspoon of yuzu zest into each bowl. Mix to incorporate.

2. In a small bowl, mix the bamboo shoots with the soy sauce.

3. In a large stockpot over medium-high heat, bring the stock and the kombu dashi to a simmer.

4. While the stock is heating, prepare a large bowl of cold water and ice.

5. Fill a medium saucepan three-quarters full of water and bring it to a rolling boil over high heat. Cook each noodle portion, separately, for about 1 minute, then place it in the ice-water bath.

6. Ladle 2 cups of broth into each bowl and mix well. Just before serving, dunk each portion of noodles back into the boiling water, shake off any excess water, and place it in the bowl. Garnish each bowl with one-quarter of the tofu slices, bamboo shoots, and scallions, and the remaining yuzu zest. Place the nori along the edge of the bowl, partially submerged.

SUBSTITUTION TIP: You can also use a combination of freshly squeezed orange and lime juice as a substitute for yuzu.

# Hakodate Shio Ramen (Traditional Hokkaido Ramen)

*Serves:* **4**          *Prep time:* **10 minutes**          *Cook time:* **50 minutes**

Hakodate, a city in snowy Hokkaido, Japan's northernmost island, has been a busy port city for thousands of years and was the first to open to foreign trade. It is also one of the very first places where ramen became popular and has become known as northern Japan's shio ramen hotspot. This recipe uses the flavor of kombu dashi to capture the city's famous ocean aromas; adding dried shiitake mushrooms to the broth deepens the flavor.

4 tablespoons Infused
Scallion Oil (page 39)

4 tablespoons Shio Citrus
Tare (page 33)

4 teaspoons mushroom
broth powder

8 cups Kombu Dashi
(page 24)

2 cups dried shiitake
mushrooms

1 package bamboo shoots

2 teaspoons light
soy sauce

1¼ pounds (3 cups or
560g) fresh ramen
noodles, store-bought or
homemade (page 46),
divided into 4 portions

1 block Twice-Thawed and
Baked Tofu (page 51)

¾ cup Seasoned Wilted
Spinach (page 53)

1 teaspoon toasted
sesame seeds

1.  Ladle 1 tablespoon of infused scallion oil, 1 tablespoon of shio citrus tare, and 1 teaspoon of mushroom broth powder into each bowl. Mix to incorporate.

2.  In a large stockpot over medium-high heat, bring the dashi to a low simmer. Add the dried mushrooms to the pot, cover, and reduce the heat to low. Simmer for 45 minutes, until the mushrooms rehydrate, turn dark brown, and are very soft.

3.  In a small bowl, mix the bamboo shoots with the soy sauce.

4.  While the stock is heating, prepare a large bowl of cold water and ice.

5.  Fill a medium saucepan three-quarters full of water and bring it to a rolling boil over high heat. Cook each noodle portion, separately, for about 1 minute, then place it in the ice-water bath.

6.  Remove the mushrooms from the broth and discard. Ladle 2 cups of broth into each bowl and mix well. Just before serving, dunk each portion of noodles back into the boiling water, shake off any excess water, and place in the bowl. Garnish each bowl with tofu, bamboo shoots, spinach, and sesame seeds.

# Simple Shoyu Ramen

*Serves:* **4**  *Prep time:* **10 minutes**  *Cook time:* **20 minutes**

In this recipe, we strip a bowl of shoyu ramen down to its bare essentials to showcase the delicious soy sauce flavor in our tare. It is slightly less involved than some of the other ramen recipes in the book, and this simplicity allows each of the soup's components to shine.

4 tablespoons Infused Garlic Oil (page 38)

4 tablespoons Shoyu Tare (page 32)

4 tablespoons light soy sauce

6 cups Vegan "Chicken" Stock (page 25)

2 cups Kombu Dashi (page 24)

1¼ pounds (3 cups or 560g) fresh ramen noodles, store-bought or homemade (page 46), divided into 4 portions

3 scallions, thinly sliced crosswise

Toasted sesame seeds, for garnish

1 sheet toasted nori, cut into 4 (2-by-4-inch) pieces

1. Ladle 1 tablespoon of infused garlic oil, 1 tablespoon of shoyu tare, and 1 tablespoon of soy sauce into each bowl. Mix to incorporate.

2. In a large stockpot over medium-high heat, bring the stock and the kombu dashi to a low simmer.

3. While the stock is heating, prepare a large bowl of cold water and ice.

4. Fill a medium saucepan three-quarters full of water and bring it to a rolling boil over high heat. Cook each noodle portion, separately, for about 1 minute, then place it in the ice-water bath.

5. Ladle 2 cups of hot broth into each bowl and mix well. Just before serving, dunk each portion of noodles back into the boiling water, shake off any excess water, and place it in the bowl. Garnish with the scallions, sesame seeds, and nori.

# Tonyu Shoyu Ramen (Creamy Soy Milk Shoyu Ramen)

*Serves: 4*  *Prep time: 15 minutes*  *Cook time: 20 minutes*

*Tonyu* means "soy milk" in Japanese. This shoyu bowl triples down on soy's savory punch with a soy sauce base, a broth that incorporates creamy soy milk, and a topping of twice-baked tofu. This recipe is inspired by a ramen spot in Portland, Oregon, Kinboshi Ramen, where Chef Mayumi Hijikata offers a tonyu bowl as her vegan ramen option.

2 tablespoons toasted sesame seeds, plus 2 teaspoons for garnish

4 tablespoons toasted sesame oil

4 tablespoons Shoyu Tare (page 32)

4 cups Vegan "Chicken" Stock (page 25)

2 cups Kombu Dashi (page 24)

2 cups plain, unsweetened soy milk

1¼ pounds (3 cups or 560g) fresh ramen noodles, store-bought or homemade (page 46), divided into 4 portions

1½ cups Garlic-Oil Corn (page 52)

1 cup Seasoned Wilted Spinach (page 53)

1 block Twice-Thawed and Baked Tofu (page 51), sliced

1. Grind 2 tablespoons of sesame seeds in a mortar and pestle or a spice grinder until they are crushed into a fine paste (some unevenness is fine).

2. Prepare 4 bowls by adding 1 tablespoon of sesame oil, 1 tablespoon of shoyu tare, and ½ tablespoon of ground sesame seeds to each. Mix to incorporate.

3. In a large stockpot over medium-high heat, bring the stock, the kombu dashi, and the soy milk to a low simmer.

4. While the stock is heating, prepare a large bowl of cold water and ice.

5. Fill a medium saucepan three-quarters full of water and bring it to a rolling boil over high heat. Cook each noodle portion, separately, for about 1 minute, then place it in the ice-water bath.

6. Ladle 2 cups of hot broth into each bowl and mix well. Just before serving, dunk each portion of noodles back into the boiling water, shake off any excess water, and place it in the bowl. Garnish each bowl with one-quarter of the corn, spinach, tofu, and remaining 2 teaspoons of sesame seeds.

# Plant-Based Tonkotsu Ramen

*Serves: 4*        *Prep time: 60 minutes*        *Cook time: 20 minutes*

Tonkotsu ramen is an anomaly, as it is the only version that isn't defined by its tare. It is also extremely popular, on par with shio, miso, and shoyu ramens. Our vegan interpretation of tonkotsu ramen (which is traditionally made through a long and labor-intensive process of boiling pork bones) is far simpler than the original. We simulate its umami and its creamy texture by combining a variety of tare, oils, and stock.

6 teaspoons Spicy Miso Tare (page 34)

6 teaspoons Shoyu Tare (page 32)

4 tablespoons Infused Garlic Oil (page 38)

6 cups Caramelized Cabbage Stock (page 26)

2 cups Kombu Dashi (page 24)

1¼ pounds (3 cups or 560g) fresh ramen noodles, store-bought or homemade (page 46), divided into 4 portions

3 to 5 scallions, thinly sliced crosswise

1 block Twice-Thawed and Baked Tofu (page 51)

Toasted nori, cut into 4 (2-by-4-inch) pieces

1. Prepare 4 bowls by adding 1½ teaspoons of miso tare, 1½ teaspoons of shoyu tare, and 1 tablespoon of garlic oil to each. Mix to incorporate.

2. In a large stockpot over medium-high heat, bring the stock and the kombu dashi to a simmer.

3. While the stock is heating, prepare a large bowl of cold water and ice.

4. Fill a medium saucepan three-quarters full of water and bring it to a rolling boil over high heat. Cook each noodle portion, separately, for about 1 minute, then place it in the ice-water bath.

5. Ladle 2 cups of hot broth into each bowl and mix well. Just before serving, dunk each portion of noodles back into the boiling water, shake off any excess water, and place it in the bowl. Garnish each bowl with one-quarter of the scallions, tofu, and nori.

# SIMPLE MISO RAMEN

*Serves:* **4**          *Prep time:* **10 minutes**          *Cook time:* **20 minutes**

Many Americans are familiar with the miso soup that comes with sushi—generally a small bowl of thin, oversalted broth. Although its base ingredient is the same, miso ramen could not be further from that appetizer. It is the heaviest and most decadent of the three primary tare bases, due to its ability to hold oil so well. This version of miso ramen keeps it simple, allowing the flavor of the miso to shine.

**4 tablespoons Spicy Miso Tare (page 34)**

**2 tablespoons white miso paste**

**6 tablespoons Infused Scallion Oil (page 39)**

**4 cups Kombu Dashi (page 24)**

**4 cups Caramelized Cabbage Stock (page 26)**

**1¼ pounds (3 cups or 560g) fresh ramen noodles, store-bought or homemade (page 46), divided into 4 portions**

**2 cups Garlic-Oil Corn (page 52)**

**3 scallions, thinly sliced crosswise**

1. Prepare 4 bowls by adding 1 tablespoon of miso tare, ½ tablespoon of white miso paste, and 1½ tablespoons of scallion oil to each. Mix to incorporate.

2. In a large stockpot over medium-high heat, bring the dashi and the stock to a simmer.

3. While the stock is heating, prepare a large bowl of cold water and ice.

4. Fill a medium saucepan three-quarters full of water and bring it to a rolling boil over high heat. Cook each noodle portion, separately, for about 1 minute, then place it in the ice-water bath.

5. Ladle 2 cups of hot broth into each bowl and mix well. Just before serving, dunk each portion of noodles back into the boiling water, shake off any excess water, and place it in the bowl. Garnish each bowl with one-quarter of the corn and scallions.

# Sapporo-Style Miso Ramen

*Serves: 4*　　　　*Prep time: **10 minutes***　　　　*Cook time: **20 minutes***

In Sapporo, on the northern island of Hokkaido, where winter is marked by cold and snow, ramen is both a delicious meal and an essential tool for warming up. You'll find this variation of a miso ramen uses significantly more oil than others; in addition to mixing the hot chili oil with the tare at the bottom of each bowl, you also drizzle on additional oil at the end for an added punch. If you want to eat like you're in Hokkaido, start here. For maximum authenticity, enjoy this ramen with a Sapporo beer.

**4 tablespoons Spicy Miso Tare (page 34)**

**2 tablespoons red miso paste**

**8 tablespoons Infused Chili Oil (page 40), divided**

**4 cups Kombu Dashi (page 24)**

**4 cups Vegan Demiglace (page 28)**

**1¼ pounds (3 cups or 560g) fresh ramen noodles, store-bought or homemade (page 46), divided into 4 portions**

**2 cups Garlic-Oil Corn (page 52)**

**3 scallions, thinly sliced crosswise**

**1 cup bean sprouts**

**1 block Twice-Thawed and Baked Tofu, sliced (page 51)**

1. Prepare 4 bowls by adding 1 tablespoon of miso tare, ½ tablespoon of red miso paste, and 1 tablespoon of chili oil to each. Mix to incorporate.

2. In a large stockpot over medium-high heat, bring the dashi and the vegan demiglace to a simmer.

3. While the stock is heating, prepare a large bowl of cold water and ice.

4. Fill a medium saucepan three-quarters full of water and bring it to a rolling boil over high heat. Cook each noodle portion, separately, for about 1 minute, then place it in the ice-water bath.

5. Ladle 2 cups of hot broth into each bowl and mix well. Just before serving, dunk each portion of noodles back into the boiling water, shake off any excess water, and place it in the bowl. Garnish each bowl with one-quarter of the corn, scallions, bean sprouts, and tofu, then drizzle on the remaining 4 tablespoons of chili oil (1 tablespoon per bowl).

# Tantanmen
# (Spicy Sesame Miso Ramen)

*Serves:* **4**          *Prep time:* **15 minutes**          *Cook time:* **20 minutes**

Tantanmen is a Japanese take on Sichuan dan dan noodles. Here we've created a vegan version that uses our Spicy Miso Tare to full effect by combining it with tahini and chili oil. Tantanmen is often served with a meat mince (like the original dan dan noodles); here we use our flavorful Soy Curl "Chicken" to create that hearty, meaty sauce.

4 tablespoons Spicy Miso Tare (page 34)

4 tablespoons tahini

4 tablespoons Infused Chili Oil (page 40), plus more for drizzling

4 servings Soy Curl "Chicken" (page 54)

2 tablespoons toasted sesame oil

6 cups Vegan "Chicken" Stock (page 25)

2 cups Caramelized Cabbage Stock (page 26)

1¼ pounds (3 cups or 560g) fresh ramen noodles, store-bought or homemade (page 46), divided into 4 portions

3 scallions, thinly sliced crosswise

1 cup fresh cherry tomatoes, halved

1 cup Seasoned Wilted Spinach (page 53)

1 tablespoon toasted sesame seeds

1. Prepare 4 bowls by adding 1 tablespoon of miso tare, 1 tablespoon of tahini, and 1 tablespoon of chili oil to each. Mix to incorporate.

2. Finely mince the soy curl chicken. In a medium bowl, mix the soy curl chicken with the sesame oil.

3. In a large stockpot over medium-high heat, bring the vegan chicken stock and the caramelized cabbage stock to a simmer.

4. While the stock is heating, prepare a large bowl of cold water and ice.

5. Fill a medium saucepan three-quarters full of water and bring it to a rolling boil over high heat. Cook each noodle portion, separately, for about 1 minute, then place it in the ice-water bath.

6. Ladle 2 cups of hot broth into each bowl and mix well. Just before serving, dunk each portion of noodles back into the boiling water, shake off any excess water, and place in the bowl. Garnish each bowl with one-quarter of the soy curls, scallions, tomatoes, spinach, and sesame seeds. Drizzle on more chili oil, if you like.

SUBSTITUTION TIP: If you don't have tahini on hand, you can use unsalted peanut butter in a pinch.

# KIMCHI RAMEN

*Serves:* **4**             *Prep time:* **5 minutes**             *Cook time:* **30 minutes**

Kimchi—spicy, pickled, fermented vegetables—is a staple of Korean cuisine. In this popular fusion dish, kimchi and another Korean ingredient, *gochugaru*, are paired with miso for a powerfully flavorful bowl of ramen. (Many kinds of kimchi are made with dried fish; check the ingredients list carefully when purchasing.)

4 tablespoons Spicy Miso
  Tare (page 34)

4 tablespoons Infused
  Chili Oil (page 40)

1 (16-ounce) jar cab-
  bage kimchi

4 cups Kombu Dashi
  (page 24)

4 cups Caramelized Cab-
  bage Stock (page 26)

1¼ pounds (3 cups or
  560g) fresh ramen
  noodles, store-bought or
  homemade (page 46),
  divided into 4 portions

3 scallions, thinly sliced
  crosswise

1 teaspoon Korean
  red pepper flakes
  (gochugaru)

1 teaspoon toasted
  sesame seeds

1.  Prepare 4 bowls by adding 1 tablespoon of miso tare, 1 tablespoon of chili oil, and 2 tablespoons of kimchi juice to each. Mix to incorporate.

2.  In a large stockpot over medium-high heat, bring the dashi and the stock to a simmer.

3.  While the stock is heating, prepare a large bowl of cold water and ice.

4.  Fill a medium saucepan three-quarters full of water and bring it to a rolling boil over high heat. Cook each noodle portion, separately, for about 1 minute, then place it in the ice-water bath.

5.  Ladle 2 cups of hot broth into each bowl and mix well. Just before serving, dunk each portion of noodles back into the boiling water, shake off any excess water, and place it in the bowl. Garnish each bowl with one-quarter of the kimchi (without its liquid), scallions, red pepper flakes, and sesame seeds.

# Japanese-Style Curry Ramen

*Serves:* **4**    *Prep time:* **10 minutes**    *Cook time:* **40 minutes**

Japanese-style curry is usually eaten with rice, but by swapping one carb for another—rice for ramen noodles—we create a whole new textural experience. S&B is one of the most popular curry brands outside of Japan and is widely available in most major grocery stores. By using their premade sauce mix as a shortcut, we can easily build a complex, spicy, and umami-filled base for our ramen.

4 tablespoons Shoyu Tare (page 32)

2 tablespoons Infused Garlic Oil (page 38)

1 yellow potato, cubed

2 medium carrots, diced

1 medium yellow onion, diced

3 blocks S&B Golden Curry Sauce Mix (medium heat)

8 cups Kombu Dashi (page 24)

1 cup snow peas

1¼ pounds (3 cups or 560g) fresh ramen noodles, store-bought or homemade (page 46), divided into 4 portions

2 to 3 scallions, thinly sliced crosswise

1. Prepare 4 ramen bowls by ladling 1 tablespoon of shoyu tare into each.

2. In a large stockpot over medium-low heat, heat the infused garlic oil. Once it is hot, add the potato, carrot, and onion, and cook, stirring frequently, until they begin to soften, about 30 minutes.

3. Add the curry roux and cook it until the vegetables are coated. Add the dashi and the snow peas. Cover the pot and bring the broth to a simmer, and cook for about 10 minutes.

4. While the vegetables are cooking, prepare a large bowl of cold water and ice.

5. Fill a medium saucepan three-quarters full of water and bring it to a rolling boil over high heat. Cook each noodle portion, separately, for about 1 minute, then place it in the ice-water bath.

6. Ladle 2 cups of hot soup and one-quarter of the vegetables into each bowl and mix well. Just before serving, dunk each portion of noodles back into the boiling water, shake off any excess water, and place in the bowl. Garnish each bowl with one-quarter of the scallions.

# THAI RED CURRY RAMEN

*Serves:* **4**          *Prep time:* **5 minutes**          *Cook time:* **25 minutes**

In this recipe, we've taken the principles behind Japanese curry and combined them with the distinctive flavors of Thai red curry paste to create a uniquely delicious ramen. The curry's medley of complex spices shines through and is heightened by the umami of miso tare. The Caramelized Cabbage Stock is a perfect rich and creamy base, while brown sugar adds a bit of sweetness and serves to heighten the other flavors.

4 tablespoons Spicy Miso Tare (page 34)

4 tablespoons Infused Chili Oil (page 40)

2 tablespoons Thai red curry paste

2 teaspoons curry powder

6 cups Caramelized Cabbage Stock (page 26)

2 cups Kombu Dashi (page 24)

¼ cup light brown sugar

1¼ pounds (3 cups or 560g) fresh ramen noodles, store-bought or homemade (page 46), divided into 4 portions

4 tablespoons full-fat coconut cream

1 cup Seared Mushrooms (page 49)

1 block Fried Sweet-Glaze Tofu (page 50)

½ bunch cilantro, roughly chopped

2 teaspoons toasted sesame seeds

1 lime, quartered

1. Prepare 4 bowls by adding 1 tablespoon of miso tare, 1 tablespoon of infused chili oil, ½ tablespoon of curry paste, and ½ teaspoon of curry powder to each. Mix to incorporate.

2. In a large stockpot over medium-high heat, bring the stock and the dashi to a simmer. Add the sugar and stir until it has dissolved.

3. While the stock is heating, prepare a large bowl of cold water and ice.

4. Fill a medium saucepan three-quarters full of water and bring it to a rolling boil over high heat. Cook each noodle portion, separately, for about 1 minute, then place it in the ice-water bath.

5. Ladle 2 cups of hot broth into each bowl and mix well. Just before serving, dunk each portion of noodles back into the boiling water, shake off any excess water, and place it in the bowl. Garnish each bowl with a drizzle of coconut cream; one quarter of the mushrooms, tofu, cilantro, and sesame seeds; and a lime wedge.

# Tsukemen (Dipping Ramen)

*Serves: **4***       *Prep time: **10 minutes***       *Cook time: **40 minutes***

This dish has all our usual ramen elements, but the broth is concentrated and separated into another bowl. To eat the ramen, you dip each mouthful of noodles into the broth separately. (The word *tsuke* means "dip.") To turn this broth into a flavorful dip, we use less stock and more tare. Unlike most ramen recipes, this dish is best when the noodles are served lukewarm (though the broth should still be piping hot). Grab some noodles from their bowl with chopsticks, submerge them in the dip until they're coated, and slurp them down.

8 tablespoons Shoyu Tare (page 32)

6 tablespoons Infused Garlic Oil (page 38)

5 cups Vegan "Chicken" Stock (page 25)

1¼ pounds (3 cups or 560g) fresh ramen noodles, store-bought or homemade (page 46), divided into 4 portions

3 scallions, thinly sliced crosswise

1 cup Seared Mushrooms (page 49)

1 block Twice-Thawed and Baked Tofu (page 51), sliced

2 teaspoons toasted sesame seeds

1. Prepare 4 small bowls of dip by adding 2 tablespoons of shoyu tare and 1 tablespoon of garlic oil to each. Mix to incorporate. Prepare 4 larger bowls by adding ½ tablespoon of the remaining garlic oil to each.

2. In a large stockpot over medium-high heat, bring the stock to a boil. Boil the stock until it has reduced by at least one cup of liquid, about 20 minutes, then remove the pot from the heat.

3. Fill a medium saucepan three-quarters full of water and bring it to a rolling boil over high heat. Cook each noodle portion, separately, for about 1 minute, then run them under cool water to stop the cooking process; they should still be lukewarm.

4. Ladle 1 cup of hot broth into each small bowl, mixing well. Divide the cooked noodles among the larger bowls, and mix each portion with the garlic oil, to prevent them from sticking to each other. Garnish each bowl of noodles with one-quarter of the scallions, mushrooms, tofu, and sesame seeds, and serve the noodles and the dip side by side.

# Hiyashi Chuka (Cold Summer Ramen)

*Serves: 3*     *Prep time: 1 hour*     *Cook time: 5 minutes*

This brothless ramen is crisp and refreshing. The noodles are dressed with sesame oil and soy sauce, and topped with quick-pickled veggies. While hiyashi chuka is usually served with ham and eggs, this recipe uses fried tofu.

6 tablespoons light soy sauce

3 tablespoons toasted sesame oil

4 tablespoons rice vinegar, divided

1 tablespoon lime juice

1 tablespoon light brown sugar

½ teaspoon grated ginger

1 tablespoon sea salt

1 tablespoon granulated sugar

2 carrots, thinly sliced

½ daikon radish, peeled and thinly sliced

1 pound (2¼ cups or 420g) fresh ramen noodles, store-bought or homemade (page 46), divided into 3 portions

1 block Fried Sweet-Glaze Tofu (page 50)

1 medium cucumber, thinly sliced crosswise

¼ head purple cabbage, cored and thinly sliced

1 tablespoon toasted sesame seeds

1. In a medium bowl, whisk the soy sauce, sesame oil, 1 tablespoon of rice vinegar, the lime juice, the brown sugar, and the ginger to combine into a dressing. Cover the bowl and refrigerate.

2. In a zip-top bag, mix the remaining 3 tablespoons of rice vinegar, the salt, and the granulated sugar. Add the carrot and daikon, massaging the vegetables to coat them in the pickling solution. Press the air out of the bag, seal it, and refrigerate for 45 minutes to pickle.

3. Prepare a large bowl of cold water and ice.

4. Fill a medium saucepan three-quarters full of water and bring it to a rolling boil over high heat. Cook each noodle portion, separately, for about 1 minute, then place it in the ice-water bath.

5. Mix each cold noodle portion in a mixing bowl with 3 tablespoons of the dressing, then transfer it to a plate. Repeat with all the portions of noodles. Drain the carrots and daikon, discarding the pickling solution. Arrange one-quarter of the pickled carrots and daikon, tofu, cucumber, and cabbage on top of each plate of noodles and drizzle on any remaining dressing. Garnish the dishes with toasted sesame seeds.

SUBSTITUTION TIP: The vegetables in this dish are completely customizable; use any veggies you've already got sitting in your refrigerator.

# TANMEN
# (RAMEN WITH STIR-FRIED VEGETABLES)

***

*Serves:* **4**   *Prep time:* **20 minutes**   *Cook time:* **30 minutes**

This style of ramen, distinctive for its stir-fried vegetable topping, is popular in the Kanto region of Japan. While the cooking process for this ramen is unconventional—the vegetables are partially cooked in the soup before serving—the end result is no less delicious.

2 teaspoons finely grated ginger

4 teaspoons Shio Citrus Tare (page 33)

4 tablespoons Infused Garlic Oil (page 38)

1 leek, white part only, thinly sliced

1 medium carrot, diced

¼ head green cabbage, cored and thickly sliced

1 teaspoon sea salt

¼ teaspoon ground white pepper

8 cups Vegan "Chicken" Stock (page 25)

1¼ pounds (3 cups or 560g) fresh ramen noodles, store-bought or homemade (page 46), divided into 4 portions

1 cup Seared Mushrooms (page 49)

1½ cups bean sprouts

1. Prepare 4 bowls by ladling ½ teaspoon of ginger and 1 tablespoon of citrus shio tare into each.

2. In a large stockpot over medium-low heat, heat the garlic oil. Once hot, add the leek, carrot, and cabbage to the pot. Increase the heat to high and stir-fry for 6 to 7 minutes, stirring frequently, until the vegetables are crispy brown and tender. Season with the salt and pepper.

3. Add the stock and bring the mixture to a boil over medium-high heat. Once it's boiling, cook the mixture for 15 minutes, until the vegetables are soft.

4. While the stock is heating, prepare a large bowl of cold water and ice.

5. Fill a medium saucepan three-quarters full of water and bring it to a rolling boil over high heat. Cook each noodle portion, separately, for about 1 minute, then place it in the ice-water bath.

6. Ladle 2 cups of hot broth and one-quarter of the vegetables into each bowl and mix well. Just before serving, dunk each portion of noodles back into the boiling water, shake off any excess water, and place it in the bowl. Stir to mix the noodles with the vegetables. Garnish each bowl with one-quarter of the mushrooms and bean sprouts.

# MAZEMEN
## (BROTHLESS RAMEN)

*Serves: 4*  *Prep time: 10 minutes*  *Cook time: 25 minutes*

*Mazemen*, which translates to "mixed noodles," is a ramen bowl without any broth. Instead, the dish relies on the oil and tare, leaving you with a strong sauce and light toppings. Think of the combination of oil and tare as a sauce used to dress the noodles. It is similar to the cold, salad-like Hiyashi Chuka (page 75), but this dish is served warm.

4 tablespoons Spicy Miso Tare (page 34)

4 tablespoons Shoyu Tare (page 32)

4 tablespoons Infused Garlic Oil (page 38)

1¼ pounds (3 cups or 560g) fresh ramen noodles, store-bought or homemade (page 46), divided into 4 portions

1 cup Seared Mushrooms (page 49)

3 scallions, thinly sliced crosswise

2 tablespoon toasted sesame seeds

1 sheet toasted nori, cut into 4 (2-by-4-inch) pieces

1. Prepare 4 bowls by adding 1 tablespoon of miso tare, 1 tablespoon of shoyu tare, and 1 tablespoon of infused garlic oil to each. Mix to incorporate.

2. Fill a medium saucepan three-quarters full of water and bring it to a rolling boil over high heat. Cook each noodle portion, separately, for about 1 minute, then briefly rinse it under cool water to stop the cooking process; they should still be lukewarm.

3. Put each portion of noodles into a bowl, and vigorously stir them with the oil and tare until they're evenly coated. Garnish each bowl with one-quarter of the seared mushrooms, scallions, sesame seeds, and nori.

# Mom's "Chicken Soup" Ramen

*Serves:* **4**  *Prep time:* **10 minutes**  *Cook time:* **50 minutes**

If it *is* true that chicken noodle soup has a healing effect (and there are various studies that claim it does), then the same can be said of vegan ramen. By combining our Vegan "Chicken" Stock, Soffritto Tare, Soy Curl "Chicken", and other ingredients, we create a bowl that captures the savory, rejuvenating power of that childhood chicken soup.

8 tablespoons
  Infused Garlic Oil
  (page 38), divided
4 tablespoon Soffritto Tare
  (page 35)
Zest of 1 lemon
1 medium carrot, diced
3 stalks celery, diced
8 cups Vegan "Chicken"
  Stock (page 25)
1¼ pounds (3 cups or
  560g) fresh ramen
  noodles, store-bought or
  homemade (page 46),
  divided into 4 portions
1 cup Soy Curl "Chicken"
  (page 54)
1 scallion, thinly sliced
  crosswise
1 lemon, quartered

1. Prepare 4 bowls by adding 1 tablespoon of garlic oil, 1 tablespoon of soffritto tare, and one-quarter of the lemon zest to each. Mix to incorporate.

2. In a large stockpot over medium-low heat, heat the remaining 4 tablespoons of garlic oil. Once hot, add the carrot and celery. Cook without stirring for 5 minutes, then continue cooking, stirring occasionally, until browned and tender, about 15 minutes.

3. Add the stock to the pot, using a wooden spoon to scrape up any browned bits from the bottom of the pot. Increase the heat to high and bring the broth to a low boil, then reduce the heat to low and simmer for 20 minutes.

4. While the vegetables are simmering, prepare a large bowl of cold water and ice.

5. Fill a medium saucepan three-quarters full of water and bring it to a rolling boil over high heat. Cook each noodle portion, separately, for about 1 minute, then place it in the ice-water bath.

6. Stir the soup, then ladle 2 cups of broth and one-quarter of the vegetables into each bowl and mix well. Just before serving, dunk each portion of noodles back into the boiling water, shake off any excess water, and place it in the bowl. Garnish each bowl with one-quarter of the soy curls and scallions, and a squeeze of lemon juice.

# CHILI TOMATO RAMEN

*Serves:* **4**  *Prep time:* **60 minutes**  *Cook time:* **10 minutes**

Tomatoes are some of the most savory, umami-filled fruits out there. This recipe highlights their tangy, savory kick and bright flavor with a shoyu ramen base and a little heat from shichimi togarashi chili powder. We use three different tomato products here—paste, canned, and fresh—to maximize this soup's flavor.

2 tablespoons Spicy Miso Tare (page 34)

2 tablespoons Shoyu Tare (page 32)

2 tablespoons chili powder

4 teaspoons tomato paste

8 tablespoons Infused Garlic Oil (page 38), divided

6 cups Vegan "Chicken" Stock (page 25)

1 (14-ounce) can peeled, diced tomato, drained

2 tablespoons light soy sauce

4 heirloom tomatoes

¼ teaspoon sea salt

¼ teaspoon black pepper

1¼ pounds (3 cups or 560g) fresh ramen noodles, store-bought or homemade (page 46), divided into 4 portions

3 scallions, thinly sliced crosswise

4 servings Soy Curl "Chicken" (page 54)

4 teaspoons shichimi togarashi

1. Preheat the oven to broil.

2. Prepare 4 bowls by adding ½ tablespoon of miso tare, ½ tablespoon of shoyu tare, ½ tablespoon of chili powder, 1 teaspoon of tomato paste, and 1 tablespoon garlic oil to each. Mix to incorporate.

3. In a large stockpot over medium-high heat, bring the stock, the canned tomato, and the soy sauce to a simmer.

4. Cut the heirloom tomatoes in half. Transfer the halves to a large bowl and drizzle them with the remaining 4 tablespoons of garlic oil; season them with salt and pepper, and toss to coat. Place the tomatoes in a baking pan, cut-side up, and broil them on low for about 10 minutes, or just until they begin to release their juices.

5. Prepare a large bowl of cold water and ice.

6. Fill a medium saucepan three-quarters full of water and bring it to a rolling boil over high heat. Cook each noodle portion, separately, for about 1 minute, then place it in the ice-water bath.

7. Ladle 2 cups of hot broth into each bowl and mix well. Just before serving, dunk each portion of noodles back into the boiling water, shake off any excess water, and place it in the bowl. Garnish each bowl with one-quarter of the broiled tomatoes, scallions, soy curls, and shichimi togarashi.

# "CHEESE" RAMEN

*Serves: 4*          *Prep time: 5 minutes*          *Cook time: 10 minutes*

Although it may sound strange, cheese ramen really is a dish you'll find in Japan. It started as an innovation in instant ramen and then spread to regular ramen. (The American dairy industry has had a pretty substantial influence on Japanese food in a variety of ways over the years.) *Mukbang*, or online eating shows, pushed this new trend, making it pretty popular. The best American analogue is classic macaroni and cheese. In our version, we use the high saturated fat content of coconut milk to transform broth into something thicker and, for lack of a better word, cheesier.

4 tablespoons Soffritto Tare (page 35)

3 cups Vegan "Chicken" Stock (page 25)

1 cup full-fat coconut milk

2 tablespoons cornstarch

1½ cup ice-cold water

⅓ cup nutritional yeast flakes

2 tablespoons white miso

2 teaspoons freshly squeezed lemon juice

½ teaspoon garlic powder

½ teaspoon onion powder

¼ teaspoon paprika

2 cups broccoli crowns

1¼ pounds (3 cups or 560g) fresh ramen noodles, store-bought or homemade (page 46), divided into 4 portions

1. Prepare 4 bowls by ladling 1 tablespoon of soffritto tare into each.

2. In a large stockpot over medium-high heat, bring the stock and the coconut milk to a simmer.

3. While the stock is heating, prepare a large bowl of cold water and ice.

4. Fill a medium saucepan three-quarters full of water and bring it to a rolling boil over high heat.

5. Create a slurry by mixing the cornstarch and ice-cold water, whisking until there are no lumps. Add the nutritional yeast, miso, lemon juice, garlic powder, onion powder, and paprika, and mix well. When the stock comes to a rolling boil, add the slurry to the broth, stirring until it thickens slightly, about 2 minutes, then remove the pot from the heat.

6. When the pot of water comes to a boil, add the broccoli and blanch it for 1 minute for a firm texture or 2 minutes for more tender florets. Using a slotted spoon, transfer the broccoli to the ice-water bath.

7. Cook each noodle portion, separately, in the same pot of water used to blanch the broccoli, for about 1 minute, rinsing each portion briefly with cold water as soon as it's done to halt the cooking process; the noodles should still be lukewarm.

8. Ladle 1 cup of the "cheesy" broth into each bowl, whisking with chopsticks to integrate the tare. Add the noodles, and mix well, then top each bowl with one-quarter of the broccoli.

SUBSTITUTION TIP: This recipe can be made with your favorite vegan cheese instead of our homemade "cheese" sauce. Simply melt the cheese in a saucepan with a bit of stock and nondairy milk, season to taste, and use it in step 4.

# "BEEF STEW" RAMEN

*Serves: 4*    *Prep time: 15 minutes*    *Cook time: 1 hour, 40 minutes*

Beef stew is an American classic. With the magic trick that is our vegan demiglace stock, we can match the stew's richness and make a dense, gravy-like sauce to coat our ramen noodles. Like an actual stew, this ramen's toppings are cooked in the broth: Our Twice-Thawed and Baked Tofu serves as our "beef."

4 tablespoons Spicy Miso Tare (page 34)

4 tablespoons Infused Garlic Oil (page 38)

1 teaspoon liquid smoke

4 cups Vegan Demiglace (page 28)

4 cups Vegan "Chicken" Stock (page 25)

2 russet potatoes, peeled and cubed

2 yellow onions, diced

2 medium-size car-rots, diced

2 stalks celery, diced

1 block Twice-Thawed and Baked Tofu (page 51)

1¼ pounds (3 cups or 560g) fresh ramen noodles, store-bought or homemade (page 46), divided into 4 portions

2 teaspoons red pepper flakes

2 tablespoons chives, thinly sliced

1. Prepare 4 bowls by adding 1 tablespoon of miso tare, 1 tablespoon garlic oil, and ¼ teaspoon of liquid smoke to each. Mix to incorporate.

2. In a large stockpot over medium-high heat, bring the vegan demiglace and the stock to a simmer. Add the potato, onion, carrot, celery, and tofu to the pot. Once it reaches a low boil, reduce the heat to medium-low and cook for 90 minutes, until the vegetables are tender and the broth has thickened to a stew-like texture.

3. While the stock is heating, prepare a large bowl of cold water and ice.

4. Fill a medium saucepan three-quarters full of water and bring it to a rolling boil over high heat. Cook each noodle portion, separately, for about 1 minute, then place in the ice-water bath.

5. Ladle 2 cups of hot broth and ¼ of the cooked tofu and vegetables into each bowl and mix well. Just before serving, dunk each portion of noodles back into the boiling water, shake off any excess water, and place it in the bowl. Garnish each bowl with the pepper flakes and chives.

TIP: Liquid smoke is a concentrated flavoring made from collecting smoke particles from wood chips burned at high temperatures. A couple drops instantly give anything you're cooking a wonderfully smoky flavor and aroma.

# TORI PAITAN
## (CREAMY "CHICKEN" RAMEN)

*Serves: 4*       *Prep time: 5 minutes*       *Cook time: 20 minutes*

*Tori paitan* translates to "white chicken soup." It is a cousin of the ever-popular tonkotsu ramen but uses chicken broth instead of pork. By combining our Vegan "Chicken" Stock with our Caramelized Cabbage Stock, we reach a balanced light and creamy soup texture. This bowl perfectly showcases how wonderful Soy Curl "Chicken" can be as a topping.

4 tablespoons Spicy Miso Tare (page 34)

4 tablespoons Shio Citrus Tare (page 33)

4 tablespoons Infused Garlic Oil (page 38)

4 cups Vegan "Chicken" Stock (page 25)

4 cups Caramelized Cabbage Stock (page 26)

1¼ pounds (3 cups or 560g) fresh ramen noodles, store-bought or homemade (page 46), divided into 4 portions

3 scallions, thinly sliced crosswise

2 cups Soy Curl "Chicken" (page 54)

1 bunch Italian parsley, chopped

1. Prepare 4 bowls by adding 1 tablespoon of miso tare, 1 tablespoon of shio citrus tare, and 1 tablespoon of garlic oil to each. Mix to incorporate.

2. In a large stockpot over medium-high heat, bring the vegan chicken stock and the caramelized cabbage stock to a simmer.

3. While the stock is heating, prepare a large bowl of cold water and ice.

4. Fill a medium saucepan three-quarters full of water and bring it to a rolling boil over high heat. Cook each noodle portion, separately, for about 1 minute, then place it in the ice-water bath.

5. Ladle 2 cups of hot broth into each bowl and mix well. Just before serving, dunk each portion of noodles back into the boiling water, shake off any excess water, and place it in the bowl. Garnish each bowl with one-quarter of the scallions, soy curls, and parsley.

# "KONKOTSU" RAMEN
# (SAFFRAMEN'S CORN RAMEN)

*Serves:* **4**　　　*Prep time:* **10 minutes**　　　*Cook time:* **20 minutes**

At our food cart, Safframen, we've spent the better part of two years perfecting our signature dish. We call it "konkotsu" ramen, a pun on the popular tonkotsu-style ramen and the Japanese word for "corn." Creamy, buttery, and salty, it is the perfect vessel for sweet corn kernels and juicy sliced tofu. We hope this version turns out as delicious in your kitchen as it does at our cart.

4 tablespoons Shoyu Tare (page 32)

2 tablespoons Infused Garlic Oil (page 38)

2 tablespoons Infused Scallion Oil (page 39)

8 cups Caramelized Cabbage Stock (page 26)

1¼ pounds (3 cups or 560g) fresh ramen noodles, store-bought or homemade (page 46), divided into 4 portions

3 scallions, thinly sliced crosswise

2 cups Garlic-Oil Corn (page 52)

1 block Twice-Thawed and Baked Tofu, sliced (page 51)

4 tablespoons store-bought fried onions (the unbreaded variety)

4 teaspoons sesame seeds

1. Prepare 4 bowls by adding 1 tablespoon of shoyu tare, ½ tablespoon of garlic oil, and ½ tablespoon of scallion oil to each. Mix to incorporate.

2. In a large stockpot over medium-high heat, bring the stock to a simmer.

3. While the stock is heating, prepare a large bowl of cold water and ice.

4. Fill a medium saucepan three-quarters full of water and bring it to a rolling boil over high heat. Cook each noodle portion, separately, for about 1 minute, then place it in the ice-water bath.

5. Ladle 2 cups of hot broth into each bowl and mix well. Just before serving, dunk each portion of noodles back into the boiling water, shake off any excess water, and place it in the bowl. Garnish each bowl with one-quarter of the scallions, corn, tofu, fried onions, and sesame seeds.

SUBSTITUTION TIP: You can also use this recipe to make the spicy ramen we serve at Safframen: Simply substitute Infused Chili Oil (page 40) for the garlic oil, then top the bowl with Korean red pepper flakes, Thai chili flakes, slices of fresh jalapeño, and some dried, ground red chili (the kind found in Asian grocery stores).

# Ash Reshteh Ramen (Persian Ramen Noodle Soup)

*Serves: 4*  *Prep time: 5 minutes*  *Cook time: 1 hour, 20 minutes*

When Armon was growing up, his family regularly made a wide variety of traditional Persian dishes, including ash reshteh, a thick noodle soup full of herbs and legumes. It traditionally uses a unique type of Persian noodle, called ash, which is made with enriched wheat. When Armon first became interested in ramen, part of what inspired him was seeing ramen's potential: Ramen can be anything, as long as certain principles are followed, which means that it can also be ash reshteh.

6 tablespoons Infused Garlic Oil (page 38), divided

4 tablespoons Shio Citrus Tare (page 33)

4 white onions, diced

1 teaspoon ground turmeric

4 cups Vegan "Chicken" Stock (page 25)

4 cups Kombu Dashi (page 24)

1 cup canned or cooked chickpeas, drained

1 cup canned or cooked red beans, drained

½ cup coarsely chopped cilantro, divided

¼ cup coarsely chopped fresh mint, divided

¼ cup coarsely chopped fresh dill, divided

1 cup spinach

1¼ pounds (3 cups or 560g) fresh ramen noodles, store-bought or homemade (page 46), divided into 4 portions

1.  Prepare 4 bowls by ladling 1 tablespoon of garlic oil and 1 tablespoon of shio tare into each. Mix to incorporate.

2.  In a large stockpot over medium-low heat, heat the remaining 2 tablespoons of garlic oil. Once it's hot, add the onion and sauté, stirring frequently. After 5 minutes, add the turmeric and continue cooking, stirring frequently, until the onions turn translucent, about 15 minutes.

3.  Add the stock and dashi to the stockpot, then the chickpeas and beans. Bring the soup to a simmer, then add half the cilantro, mint, and dill, and all the spinach. Cook the soup for 45 minutes at a low simmer, or until the beans are tender, the soup has thickened, and herbs begin to lose their color.

4.  While the stock is heating, prepare a large bowl of cold water and ice.

5.  Fill a medium saucepan three-quarters full of water and bring it to a rolling boil over high heat. Cook each noodle portion, separately, for about 1 minute, then place it in the ice-water bath.

6.  Ladle 2 cups of hot soup and one-quarter of the vegetables, beans, and herbs into each bowl, and mix well. Just before serving, dunk each portion of noodles back into the boiling water, shake off any excess water, and place it in the bowl. Garnish each bowl with one-quarter of the remaining cilantro, mint, and dill.

*Yuzu Lemonade,*
*page 97*

*Savory Veggie Gyoza,*
*page 90*

# CHAPTER 4
# SIDES AND DRINKS

# SAVORY VEGGIE GYOZA

*Makes: 52 gyoza*   *Prep time: 30 minutes*   *Cook time: 30 minutes*

Gyoza are one of the most popular sides you'll find in ramen joints around the world. These tender, chewy dumplings are a take on the Chinese panfried version but with Japanese influences. The Chinese version often is filled with pork and cabbage, while Japanese gyoza can be more veggie-forward. Our vegan version is bursting with mushroom, sweet carrot, leek, and scallion. We've simplified this recipe slightly by recommending store-bought dumpling wrappers. Both the gyoza filling and the gyoza themselves freeze well (and this recipe yields enough gyoza for several meals).

## FOR THE GYOZA

- 4 cups finely chopped shiitake mushroom caps
- 2 carrots, finely chopped
- ¼ head green cabbage, cored and finely chopped
- 4 or 5 scallions, finely chopped
- 1 leek, white part only, finely chopped
- ½ teaspoon sea salt
- 1 tablespoon minced ginger

- 1 tablespoon minced garlic
- 1 tablespoon light soy sauce
- 1 teaspoon toasted sesame oil, plus more for frying
- 1 tablespoon red miso
- 2 teaspoon mirin
- ½ teaspoon freshly ground black pepper
- ⅛ teaspoon ground white pepper

- 2 tablespoons cornstarch, plus extra for dusting
- ¼ cup cold water, plus more for wetting the dumpling wrappers and frying the dumplings
- 1 (52-wrapper) package gyoza wrappers (thawed if frozen)
- 3 scallions, thinly sliced crosswise, for garnish

## FOR THE DIPPING SAUCE

- 1 tablespoon soy sauce
- 2 teaspoon rice vinegar

- 1 teaspoon sesame oil

- 1 teaspoon toasted sesame seeds

1.  **To make the gyoza:** In a large bowl, combine the mushroom, carrot, cabbage, scallion, leek, and salt, and mix with a wooden spatula until the vegetables begin to soften, 5 to 8 minutes. Add the ginger, garlic, soy sauce, sesame oil, red miso, mirin, black pepper, and white pepper and mix well.

2.  In a small cup, whisk the cornstarch and water until there are no lumps. Pour the cornstarch mixture into the bowl of vegetables and mix until mixture is dry enough to hold together and form loose balls of filling. (Add more cornstarch as needed.)

3.  Dust the surface of a cutting board with cornstarch. Place a small bowl of cold water next to the board. Take a gyoza wrapper, place it in the palm of your hand, and spoon a tablespoon of filling into the center. Dip your finger in the water and wet the edges of the wrapper, then fold the wrapper in half to enclose the filling and press down along the edges to seal. Make sure all the air is pressed out of the wrapper before tightly sealing. (Optional step: To create pleats, use your thumb and index finger to make folds along the edge of the wrapper.) Place the gyoza on the cornstarch-dusted surface. Repeat this step until you've used all of the remaining wrappers and filling.

4.  Fry the gyoza in batches: In a large skillet or saucepan with a lid, heat 1 to 2 tablespoons of sesame oil on medium-low heat. Once it's hot, use tongs to place the gyoza into the pan, flat-side down, making sure not to crowd the pan. Fry the gyoza, uncovered, for about 3 minutes, or until the bottoms are golden brown.

5.  Add ¼ cup of water to the pan and quickly cover it. When the water has evaporated, after about 1 minute, remove the lid and drizzle an additional 1 teaspoon of sesame oil over the gyoza. Cook for 2 more minutes, or until the bottoms are crisp, then transfer the gyoza to a serving plate and garnish them with sliced scallions. Repeat steps 4 and 5 until all the gyoza are cooked. (Alternatively, you can freeze your filled, uncooked gyoza in an airtight bag, in a single layer. The gyoza can be cooked from frozen, steamed a minute or two longer to soften the filling.)

6.  **To make the dipping sauce:** In a small bowl, whisk together the soy sauce, rice vinegar, sesame oil, and toasted sesame seeds. Serve alongside the gyoza.

COOKING TIP: Fry your gyoza delicately in the pan and don't move them around too much once they're sizzling; the wrappers tend to break open if mishandled. Carefully check them after 3 minutes. If the bottoms are golden brown, they will no longer stick to the pan.

# SUNOMONO SALAD

*Serves:* **4**     *Prep time:* **5 minutes**

Light and refreshing, this cucumber salad pairs perfectly with a rich bowl of ramen, balancing the intense flavors of the soup. Fresh, quick-pickled cucumbers are somewhat unique in Asian cuisines and have a more mellow flavor than other pickles. Japanese or Persian cucumbers work best for this recipe, but English cucumbers will also work well.

3 cups thinly sliced cucumber rounds

2 teaspoons sea salt

3 tablespoons rice vinegar

1 tablespoon light soy sauce

1 teaspoon toasted sesame oil

1 tablespoon granulated sugar

1 teaspoon toasted sesame seeds

1. In a medium bowl, mix the cucumbers with the salt. Set the bowl aside and let the cucumbers soften for at least 5 minutes.

2. Meanwhile, in a small bowl, combine the rice vinegar, soy sauce, toasted sesame oil, and sugar, and mix everything until the sugar has dissolved.

3. Add the dressing to the cucumbers and toss until they are evenly coated. Drain the excess liquid. Transfer the cucumbers to a serving plate, and garnish them with the sesame seeds.

COOKING TIP: The longer the cucumbers sit in the dressing, the more intense their flavor will be, so it's best to prepare this dish ahead of time and refrigerate it until you're ready to serve.

# PANFRIED EDAMAME

*Serves:* **4**          *Prep time:* **2 minutes**          *Cook time:* **20 minutes**

This recipe is more proof of the endless utility of soy. These boiled young soybean pods are a staple in *izakayas* (pubs) and *konbini* (convenience stores) across Japan. They make a quick and easy snack and pair beautifully with cold Asahi beer and a piping-hot bowl of ramen. The edamame pods are cooked and served whole so diners can remove each bean as they eat.

**3 cups frozen
edamame in pods**
**3 tablespoons toasted
sesame oil**
**1 tablespoon light
soy sauce**
**1 garlic clove, finely
minced (optional)**
**Pinch sea salt**

1. Fill a medium saucepan halfway with water and bring it to a boil. Add the edamame pods and boil them for 3 to 4 minutes, then drain them and run them under cold tap water until they are cooled. Pat the pods dry with a clean kitchen towel.

2. In a medium skillet over medium-low heat, heat the sesame oil. Once hot, add the edamame pods and cook, stirring often, for 2 to 3 minutes, until the pods begin to brown and crisp.

3. Add the soy sauce and garlic (if using) and continue to cook everything, stirring often, until the liquid has evaporated. Turn off the heat, sprinkle the edamame with salt to taste, and serve whole.

COOKING TIP: Since the edamame are getting a hit of salt in the soy sauce, the finishing salt is mostly for appearance and texture. Use a coarse-grain or flaky salt for a picture-perfect finish.

# UMEBOSHI ONIGIRI

*Makes: **6 onigiri***          *Prep time: **10 minutes***          *Cook time: **30 minutes***

Onigiri are small, savory, triangular rice balls, usually containing some type of filling and/ or topping. They are ubiquitous in Japanese convenience stores. Umeboshi are salted, pickled plums with an intensely sour flavor. Sour pickled plums may not sound delicious to the uninitiated, but pairing them with rice neutralizes much of their mouth-puckering intensity. They are the perfect choice for filling an onigiri. Look for umeboshi in the refrigerated section of your Asian grocer. They come in wide, clear, plastic jars. The onigiri are finished wrapped in a sheet of sushi nori.

2 cups Calrose rice, Japanese sushi rice, arborio, or other short-grain rice

2 cups cold water

1 teaspoon sea salt

½ teaspoon granulated sugar

½ teaspoon rice vinegar

1 tablespoon toasted sesame seeds

1 sheet toasted, seasoned nori

1 jar umeboshi, containing at least 6 pickled plums

1. Put the rice in a colander and thoroughly rinse it under cold water until the water runs mostly clear (this washes away the starch).

2. Transfer the rice to a small saucepan and add the water (the water-to-rice ratio should be 1:1). Bring the mixture to a boil over medium-high heat, then reduce the heat to low, cover the pot, and cook. After 10 minutes, remove the saucepan from the heat but do not remove the lid. Let the rice continue steaming for 10 more minutes.

3. Transfer the cooked rice to a wide, shallow bowl or dish and spread it into an even layer. Add the salt, sugar, rice vinegar, and sesame seeds, and mix to incorporate.

4. Cut the nori into 6 (2-inch-by-4-inch) strips, for wrapping.

5. Remove the pits from 6 umeboshi.

6. Once the rice has cooled enough to be handled with bare hands, separate it into 6 equal portions.

7. Slightly wet your hands with water to keep the rice from sticking (or put on disposable, non-powdered gloves). Take one portion of rice and use your palm as a base to mold it into a flat, round shape. Create a divot with your thumb in the center of the rice, add one umeboshi to the center, then carefully close the edges of the rice around it. When the umeboshi is completely sealed in the rice, use both hands to form the rice into a thick, even triangle. (If forming the triangle is difficult, you can lay the onigiri on a damp cutting board to keep one side secure while you press it into shape.) Repeat with the remaining rice and umeboshi

8. Wrap each onigiri with one strip of the toasted nori, setting the bottom of the triangle in the center of the strip and folding the ends up and over the flat, wide sides.

# TOFU KARAAGE WITH SPICY VEGAN MAYO

*Serves:* **2**    *Prep time:* **15 minutes, plus 25 minutes to marinate**    *Cook time:* **15 minutes**

Karaage rivals edamame for the title of Japan's favorite late-night izakaya snack. This dish consists of bite-size pieces of chicken fried to crispy perfection, typically served with a slice of lemon or a squeeze of Kewpie mayonnaise (a brand of Japanese mayo that is a lot more tangy than American mayo). This recipe spares the bird and uses our twice-thawed tofu. It also includes a tweak to make your vegan mayo taste just like Kewpie.

4 tablespoons vegan mayonnaise

1 tablespoon light soy sauce

1 teaspoon mushroom powder

½ teaspoon freshly squeezed lemon juice

2 tablespoons cornstarch

2 tablespoons all-purpose flour

2 teaspoons sea salt

1 (16-ounce) block Twice-Thawed and Baked Tofu (page 51), cut into 1-inch pieces

4 cups canola oil

Lemon slices, for garnish

Parsley sprigs, for garnish

1. In a small bowl, whisk together the vegan mayonnaise, soy sauce, mushroom powder, and lemon juice; cover the bowl and refrigerate until ready to serve.

2. In a medium bowl, mix together the cornstarch, flour, and salt. Toss each piece of tofu in the mixture to coat it, adding more flour or cornstarch as necessary to ensure all the tofu is coated. (An uneven coating is fine; this will give the karaage its signature texture while frying.)

3. In a shallow pot, heat the oil on medium-high until it reaches 325°F. Using tongs, add no more than 6 pieces of battered tofu to the pot. Fry the tofu until it's deep golden brown on all sides, about 4 minutes per batch. Transfer the tofu to a wire rack. Repeat the process with the remaining tofu; you'll have about 3 batches. If desired, you can add a light sprinkle of salt to the tofu as soon as it comes out of the frying oil.

4. Serve the tofu with the spicy mayo dip and garnish it with a lemon slice and fresh parsley.

COOKING TIP: Our favorite widely available vegan mayo brand is Just Mayo. We also like Follow Your Heart Vegenaise.

# Yuzu Lemonade

*Serves:* **8**          *Prep time:* **25 minutes**

Classic lemonade gets a unique Japanese twist when you add yuzu extract. While yuzu (Japan's most popular citrus) may not be readily available where you are, you can find yuzu extract at Japanese grocery stores.

1 cup granulated sugar

6 cups cold water, divided

¾ cup freshly squeezed lemon juice (pulp reserved, if desired)

¼ cup yuzu extract

Mint leaves, for garnish

Sliced lemon peel, for garnish

1. In a small saucepan over medium-low heat, cook the sugar and 1 cup of the water, swirling the contents until the sugar is dissolved. Remove the pot from the heat and allow the simple syrup to cool to room temperature.

2. In a pitcher, combine the lemon juice and yuzu extract. (You can also add some of the lemon pulp to the mixture, if desired.) Stir in the simple syrup and the remaining 5 cups of water.

3. To serve, pour the lemonade over ice and garnish it with a mint leaf and slice of lemon peel.

SUBSTITUTION TIP: You can experiment with other citrus juice, such as lime or grapefruit, as the base of this recipe. Adjust the sweetness to your preference.

# Umeshu Cocktail

*Serves: 1*  　　　　　*Prep time: 5 minutes*

Umeshu is a liqueur made from *umeboshi*—the same sour pickled plums that are used in the Umeboshi Onigiri (page 94). Combined with a punch of whiskey and a splash of fresh ginger, it makes the perfect cocktail to accompany a bowl of ramen.

1 (2-inch) piece
　ginger root
2 ounces whiskey
4 ounces umeshu liqueur
1 cup club soda, chilled

1. Peel the ginger root and thinly slice 1 or 2 pieces of ginger for garnish.

2. Grate the remaining ginger and squeeze out roughly 1 teaspoon of juice.

3. Fill a tall glass with ice. Combine the whiskey, umeshu, and ginger juice in a small glass or cocktail shaker and mix well. Pour it over the ice.

4. Top with the club soda, and stir the drink until the outside of the glass is ice cold. Garnish the drink with the ginger slices. Serve immediately.

# MEASUREMENT CONVERSIONS

| VOLUME EQUIVALENTS | U.S. STANDARD | U.S. STANDARD (OUNCES) | METRIC (APPROXIMATE) |
|---|---|---|---|
| **LIQUID** | 2 tablespoons | 1 fl. oz. | 30 mL |
| | ¼ cup | 2 fl. oz. | 60 mL |
| | ½ cup | 4 fl. oz. | 120 mL |
| | 1 cup | 8 fl. oz. | 240 mL |
| | 1½ cups | 12 fl. oz. | 355 mL |
| | 2 cups or 1 pint | 16 fl. oz. | 475 mL |
| | 4 cups or 1 quart | 32 fl. oz. | 1 L |
| | 1 gallon | 128 fl. oz. | 4 L |
| **DRY** | ⅛ teaspoon | – | 0.5 mL |
| | ¼ teaspoon | – | 1 mL |
| | ½ teaspoon | – | 2 mL |
| | ¾ teaspoon | – | 4 mL |
| | 1 teaspoon | – | 5 mL |
| | 1 tablespoon | – | 15 mL |
| | ¼ cup | – | 59 mL |
| | ⅓ cup | – | 79 mL |
| | ½ cup | – | 118 mL |
| | ⅔ cup | – | 156 mL |
| | ¾ cup | – | 177 mL |
| | 1 cup | – | 235 mL |
| | 2 cups or 1 pint | – | 475 mL |
| | 3 cups | – | 700 mL |
| | 4 cups or 1 quart | – | 1 L |
| | ½ gallon | – | 2 L |
| | 1 gallon | – | 4 L |

**OVEN TEMPERATURES**

| FAHRENHEIT | CELSIUS (APPROXIMATE) |
|---|---|
| 250°F | 120°C |
| 300°F | 150°C |
| 325°F | 165°C |
| 350°F | 180°C |
| 375°F | 190°C |
| 400°F | 200°C |
| 425°F | 220°C |
| 450°F | 230°C |

**WEIGHT EQUIVALENTS**

| U.S. STANDARD | METRIC (APPROXIMATE) |
|---|---|
| ½ ounce | 15 g |
| 1 ounce | 30 g |
| 2 ounces | 60 g |
| 4 ounces | 115 g |
| 8 ounces | 225 g |
| 12 ounces | 340 g |
| 16 ounces or 1 pound | 455 g |

# RESOURCES

**Umi Organic:** This Portland-based noodle maker is our go-to source for fresh ramen noodles. Online orders only (UmiOrganic.com).

**Sun Noodle:** This noodle maker makes fresh ramen noodles that are available in markets across the United States. You can also order their noodles online (SunNoodle.com).

**Umami Mart:** This Japanese specialty store is an excellent source for Japanese cooking tools, like noodle strainer baskets, and shelf-stable ingredients, like Japanese soy sauces and vinegars. The shop has only one outlet (in Oakland, California), but most of their products are also available online (UmamiMart.com).

**Melissa's Produce:** This large produce distributor offers a great selection of Asian vegetables and fruits. Order online (Melissas.com).

**The Japanese Pantry:** This importer offers high-quality, shelf-stable products from Japan. Online only (TheJapanesePantry.com).

# INDEX

## ACKNOWLEDGMENTS

Thank you to our grandmothers, Narumi and Mokaram, for sharing their food and their culture with us way before we were old enough to appreciate it. We owe our careers to Bryce Hooper and John Roscoe for believing in us before we knew what we were doing, and to Portland's vegan community for taking a chance on our wacky plant-based ramen.

## ABOUT THE AUTHORS

 **Armon Pakdel** and **Zoe Lichlyter** are the owners of Safframen, a vegan ramen food cart in Portland, Oregon.

Printed in the USA
CPSIA information can be obtained
at www.ICGtesting.com
CBHW050332310524
9306CB00009B/96